D1649344

THE ANTI-SLAVERY CRUSADE

TEXTBOOK EDITION

∵

THE CHRONICLES OF AMERICA SERIES
ALLEN JOHNSON
EDITOR

GERHARD R. LOMER
CHARLES W. JEFFERYS
ASSISTANT EDITORS

THE ANTI-SLAVERY CRUSADE

A CHRONICLE OF THE GATHERING STORM
BY JESSE MACY

NEW HAVEN: YALE UNIVERSITY PRESS
TORONTO: GLASGOW, BROOK & CO.
LONDON: HUMPHREY MILFORD
OXFORD UNIVERSITY PRESS

Copyright, 1919, by Yale University Press

CONTENTS

THE ANTI-SLAVERY CRUSADE

CHAPTER I

INTRODUCTION

THE Emancipation Proclamation of President Lincoln marks the beginning of the end of a long chapter in human history. Among the earliest forms of private property was the ownership of slaves. Slavery as an institution had persisted throughout the ages, always under protest, always provoking opposition, insurrection, social and civil war, and ever bearing within itself the seeds of its own destruction. Among the historic powers of the world the United States was the last to uphold slavery, and when, a few years after Lincoln's proclamation, Brazil emancipated her slaves, property in man as a legally recognized institution came to an end in all civilized countries.

Emancipation in the United States marked the

conclusion of a century of continuous debate, in which the entire history of western civilization was traversed. The literature of American slavery is, indeed, a summary of the literature of the world on the subject. The Bible was made a standard text-book both for and against slavery. Hebrew and Christian experiences were exploited in the interest of the contending parties in this crucial controversy. Churches of the same name and order were divided among themselves and became half pro-slavery and half anti-slavery.

Greek experience and Greek literature were likewise drawn into the controversy. The Greeks themselves had set the example of arguing both for and against slavery. Their practice and their prevailing teaching, however, gave support to this institution. They clearly enunciated the doctrine that there is a natural division among human beings; that some are born to command and others to obey; that it is natural to some men to be masters and to others to be slaves; that each of these classes should fulfill the destiny which nature assigns. The Greeks also recognized a difference between races and held that some were by nature fitted to serve as slaves, and others to command as masters. The defenders of American slavery

therefore found among the writings of the Greeks
their chief arguments already stated in classic
form.

Though the Romans added little to the theory
of the fundamental problem involved, their history
proved rich in practical experience. There were
times, in parts of the Roman Empire, when personal slavery either did not exist or was limited
and insignificant in extent. But the institution
grew with Roman wars and conquests. In rural districts, slave labor displaced free labor, and in the
cities servants multiplied with the concentration of
wealth. The size and character of the slave population eventually became a perpetual menace to
the State. Insurrections proved formidable, and
every slave came to be looked upon as an enemy
to the public. It is generally conceded that the
extension of slavery was a primary cause of the
decline and fall of Rome. In the American controversy, therefore, the lesson to be drawn from
Roman experience was utilized to support the
cause of free labor.

After the Middle Ages, in which slavery under
the modified form of feudalism ran its course, there
was a reversion to the ancient classical controversy.
The issue became clearly defined in the hands of

the English and French philosophers of the seventeenth and eighteenth centuries. In place of the time-honored doctrine that the masses of mankind are by nature subject to the few who are born to rule, the contradictory dogma that all men are by nature free and equal was clearly enunciated. According to this later view, it is of the very nature of spirit, or personality, to be free. All men are endowed with personal qualities of will and choice and a conscious sense of right and wrong. To subject these native faculties to an alien force is to make war upon human nature. Slavery and despotism are, therefore, in their nature but a species of warfare. They involve the forcing of men to act in violation of their true selves. The older doctrine makes government a matter of force. The strong command the weak, or the rich exercise lordship over the poor. The new doctrine makes of government an achievement of adult citizens who agree among themselves as to what is fit and proper for the good of the State and who freely observe the rules adopted and apply force only to the abnormal, the delinquent, and the defective.

Between the upholders of these contradictory views of human nature there always has been and there always must be perpetual warfare. Their difference is such as to admit of no compromise; no middle ground is possible. The conflict is indeed irresistible. The chief interest in the American crusade against slavery arises from its relation to this general world conflict between liberty and despotism.

The Athenians could be democrats and at the same time could uphold and defend the institution of slavery. They were committed to the doctrine that the masses of the people were slaves by nature. By definition, they made slaves creatures void of will and personality, and they conveniently ignored them in matters of state. But Americans living in States founded in the era of the Declaration of Independence could not be good democrats and at the same time uphold and defend the institution of slavery, for the Declaration gives the lie to all such assumptions of human inequality by accepting the cardinal axiom that all men are created equal and are endowed with certain inalienable rights, among which are life, liberty, and the pursuit of happiness. The doctrine of equality had been developed in Europe without special reference to questions of distinct race or color. But the terms, which are universal and as broad as humanity in their denotation, came to be applied to black men as well as to white men. Massachusetts embodied in her state constitution in 1780 the words, "All men are born free and equal," and the courts ruled that these words in the state constitution had the effect of liberating the slaves and of giving to them the same rights as other citizens. This is a perfectly logical application of the doctrine of the Revolution.

The African slave-trade, however, developed earlier than the doctrine of the Declaration of Independence. Negro slavery had long been an established institution in all the American colonies. Opposition to the slave-trade and to slavery was an integral part of the evolution of the doctrine of equal rights. As the colonists contended for their own freedom, they became anti-slavery in sentiment. A standard complaint against British rule was the continued imposition of the slave-trade upon the colonists against their oft-repeated protest.

In the original draft of the Declaration of Independence, there appeared the following charges against the King of Great Britain:

He has waged cruel war against human nature itself, violating its most sacred rights of life and liberty in the persons of distant people who never offended him, captivating and carrying them into slavery in another hemisphere, or to incur miserable death in their transportation thither. This piratical warfare, the opprobrium of infidel powers, is the warfare of the Christian King of Great Britain. Determined to keep open a market where men should be bought and sold, he has prostituted his negative for suppressing every legislative attempt to prohibit or to restrain this execrable commerce.

Though this clause was omitted from the document as finally adopted, the evidence is abundant that the language expressed the prevailing sentiment of the country. To the believer in liberty and equality, slavery and the slave-trade are instances of war against human nature. No one attempted to justify slavery or to reconcile it with the principles of free government. Slavery was accepted as an inheritance for which others were to blame. Colonists at first blamed Great Britain; later apologists for slavery blamed New England for her share in the continuance of the slave-trade. The fact should be clearly comprehended that the sentiments which led to the American Revolution, and later to the French Revolution in Europe, were as broad in their application as the human race itself — that there were no limitations nor

exceptions. These new principles involved a complete revolution in the previously recognized
principles of government. The French sought to
make a master-stroke at immediate achievement
and they incurred counter-revolutions and delays.
The Americans moved in a more moderate and
tentative manner towards the great achievement,
but with them also a counter-revolution finally
appeared in the rise of an influential class who, by
openly defending slavery, repudiated the principles
upon which the government was founded.

At first the impression was general, in the South
as well as in the North, that slavery was a tem-
porary institution. The cause of emancipation
was already advocated by the Society of Friends
and some other sects. A majority of the States
adopted measures for the gradual abolition of
slavery, but in other cases there proved to be industrial barriers to emancipation. Slaves were
found to be profitably employed in clearing away
the forests; they were not profitably employed in
general agriculture. A marked exception was
found in small districts in the Carolinas and Georgia where indigo and rice were produced; and
though cotton later became a profitable crop for
slave labor, it was the producers of rice and indigo

who furnished the original barrier to the immediate extension of the policy of emancipation. Representatives from their States secured the introduction of a clause into the Constitution which delayed for twenty years the execution of the will of the country against the African slave-trade. It is said that a slave imported from Africa paid for himself in a single year in the production of rice. There were thus a few planters in Georgia and the Carolinas who had an obvious interest in the prolongation of the institution of slavery and who had influence enough to secure constitutional recognition for both slavery and the slave-trade.

The principles involved were not seriously debated. In theory all were abolitionists; in practice slavery extended to all the States. In some, actual abolition was comparatively easy; in others, it was difficult. By the end of the first quarter of the nineteenth century, actual abolition had extended to the line separating Pennsylvania from Maryland. Of the original thirteen States seven became free and six remained slave.

The absence of ardent or prolonged debate upon this issue in the early history of the United States is easily accounted for. No principle of importance was drawn into the controversy; few presumed to defend slavery as a just or righteous institution. As to conduct, each individual, each neighborhood enjoyed the freedom of a large, roomy country. Even within state lines there was liberty enough. No keen sense of responsibility for a uniform state policy existed. It was therefore not difficult for those who were growing wealthy by the use of imported negroes to maintain their privileges in the State.

If the sense of active responsibility was wanting within the separate States, much more was this true of the citizens of different States. Slavery was regarded as strictly a domestic institution. Families bought and owned slaves as a matter of individual preference. None of the original colonies or States adopted slavery by law. The citizens of the various colonies became slaveholders simply because there was no law against it.[1] The abolition of slavery was at first an individual matter or a church or a state policy. When the Constitution was formulated, the separate States had been accustomed to regard themselves as possessed of sovereign powers; hence there was no occasion for the citizens of one State to have a sense of

---

[1] In the case of Georgia there was a prohibitory law, which was disregarded.

responsibility on account of the domestic institutions of other States. The consciousness of national responsibility was of slow growth, and the conditions did not then exist which favored a general crusade against slavery or a prolonged acrimonious debate on the subject, such as arose forty years later.

In many of the States, however, there were organized abolition societies, whose object was to promote the cause of emancipation already in progress and to protect the rights of free negroes. The Friends, or Quakers, were especially active in the promotion of a propaganda for universal emancipation. A petition which was presented to the first Congress in February, 1790, with the signature of Benjamin Franklin as President of the Pennsylvania Abolition Society, contained this concluding paragraph:

From a persuasion that equal liberty was originally, and is still, the birthright of all men, and influenced by the strong ties of humanity and the principles of their institutions, your memorialists conceive themselves bound to use all justifiable endeavors to loosen the bonds of slavery, and to promote the general enjoyment of the blessings of freedom. Under these impressions they earnestly entreat your attention to the subject of slavery; that you will be pleased to countenance the restoration to liberty of those unhappy men, who, alone, in this land of freemen, are groaning in servile subjection; that you will devise means for removing this inconsistency of character from the American people; that you will promote mercy and justice towards this distressed race; and that you will step to the very verge of the power vested in you for discouraging every species of traffic in the persons of our fellowmen.[1]

The memorialists were treated with profound respect. Cordial support and encouragement came from representatives from Virginia and other slave States. Opposition was expressed by members from South Carolina and Georgia. These for the most part relied upon their constitutional guaranties. But for these guaranties, said Smith, of South Carolina, his State would not have entered the Union. In the extreme utterances in opposition to the petition there is a suggestion of the revolution which was to occur forty years later.

Active abolitionists who gave time and money to the promotion of the cause were always few in numbers. Previous to 1830 abolition societies resembled associations for the prevention of cruelty to animals — in fact, in one instance at least this was made one of the professed objects. These

[1] William Goodell, *Slavery and Anti-Slavery*, p. 99.

societies labored to induce men to act in harmony
with generally acknowledged obligations, and they
had no occasion for violence or persecution. Abolitionists were distinguished for their benevolence
and their unselfish devotion to the interests of the
needy and the unfortunate. It was only when the
ruling classes resorted to mob violence and began
to defend slavery as a divinely ordained institution
that there was a radical change in the spirit of the
controversy. The irrepressible conflict between
liberty and despotism which has persisted in all
ages became manifest when slave-masters substituted the Greek doctrine of inequality and slavery
for the previously accepted Christian doctrine of
equality and universal brotherhood.

CHAPTER II

THE GEOGRAPHY OF THE CRUSADE

IT was a mere accident that the line drawn by Mason and Dixon between Pennsylvania and Maryland became known in later years as the dividing line between slavery and freedom. The six States south of that line ultimately neglected or refused to abolish slavery, while the seven Northern States became free. Vermont became a State in 1791 and Kentucky in 1792. The third State to be added to the original thirteen was Tennessee in 1796. At that time, counting the States as they were finally classified, eight were destined to be slave and eight free. Ohio entered the Union as a State in 1802, thus giving to the free States a majority of one. The balance, however, was restored in 1812 by the admission of Louisiana as a slave State. The admission of Indiana in 1816 on the one side and of Mississippi in 1817 on the other still maintained the balance: ten free States stood against ten slave

States. During the next two years Illinois and Alabama were admitted, making twenty-two States in all, still evenly divided.

The ordinance for the government of the territory north of the Ohio River, passed in 1787 and reënacted by Congress after the adoption of the Constitution, proved to be an act of great significance in its relation to the limitation of slavery. By this ordinance slavery was forever prohibited in the Northwest Territory. In the territory south of the Ohio River slavery became permanently established. The river, therefore, became an extension of the original Mason and Dixon's Line with the new meaning attached: it became a division between free and slave territory.

It was apparently at first a mere matter of chance that a balance was struck between the two classes of States. While Virginia remained a slave State, it was natural that slavery should extend into Kentucky, which had been a part of Virginia. Likewise Tennessee, being a part of North Carolina, became slave territory. When these two Territories became slave States, the equal division began. There was yet an abundance of territory both north and south to be taken into the Union and, without any special plan or agitation, States were admitted in pairs, one free and the other slave. In the meantime there was distinctly developed the idea of the possible or probable permanence of slavery in the South and of a rivalry or even a future conflict between the two sections.

When in 1819 Missouri applied for admission to the Union with a state constitution permitting slavery, there was a prolonged debate over the whole question, not only in Congress but throughout the entire country. North and South were distinctly pitted against each other with rival systems of labor. The following year Congress passed a law providing for the admission of Missouri, but, to restore the balance, Maine was separated from Massachusetts and was admitted to the Union as a State. It was further enacted that slavery should be forever prohibited from all territory of the United States north of the parallel 36° 30', that is, north of the southern boundary of Missouri. It is this part of the act which is known as the Missouri Compromise. It was accepted as a permanent limitation of the institution of slavery. By this act Mason and Dixon's Line was extended through the Louisiana Purchase. As the western boundary was then defined, slavery could still be extended into Arkansas and into a part of what is now Oklahoma, while a great empire to the north-west was reserved for the formation of free States. Arkansas became a slave State in 1836 and Michigan was admitted as a free State in the following year.

With the admission of Arkansas and Michigan, thirteen slave States were balanced by a like number of free States. The South still had Florida, which would in time become a slave State. Against this single Territory there was an immense region to the northwest, equal in area to all the slave States combined, which, according to the Ordinance of 1787 and the Missouri Compromise, had been consecrated to freedom. Foreseeing this condition, a few Southern planters began a movement for the extension of territory to the south and west immediately after the adoption of the Missouri Compromise. When Arkansas was admitted in 1836, there was a prospect of the immediate annexation of Texas as a slave State. This did not take place until nine years later, but the propaganda, the object of which was the extension of slave territory, could not be maintained by those who contended that slavery was a curse to the country. Virginia, therefore, and other border slave States, as they became committed to the policy of expansion, ceased to tolerate official public utterances against slavery.

Three more or less clearly defined sections appear in the later development of the crusade. These are the New England States, the Middle States, and the States south of North Carolina and Tennessee. In New England, few negroes were ever held as slaves, and the institution disappeared during the first years of the Republic. The inhabitants had little experience arising from actual contact with slavery. When slavery disappeared from New England and before there had been developed in the country at large a national feeling of responsibility for its continued existence, interest in the subject declined. For twenty years previous to the founding of Garrison's *Liberator* in 1831, organized abolition movements had been almost unknown in New England. In various ways the people were isolated, separated from contact with slavery. Their knowledge of this subject of discussion was academic, theoretical, acquired at second-hand.

In New York and New Jersey slaves were much more numerous than in New England. There were still slaves in considerable numbers until about 1825. The people had a knowledge of the institution from experience and observation, and there

was no break in the continuity of their organized
abolition societies. Chief among the objects of
these societies was the effort to prevent kidnapping
and to guard the rights of free negroes. For both
of these purposes there was a continuous call for
activity. Pennsylvania also had freedmen of her
own whose rights called for guardianship, as well as
many freedmen from farther south who had come
into the State.

The movement of protest and protection did not
stop at Mason and Dixon's Line, but extended far
into the South. In both North Carolina and Tennessee an active protest against slavery was at all
times maintained. In this great middle section of
the country, between New England and South
Carolina, there was no cessation in the conflict
between free and slave labor. Some of these States
became free while others remained slave; but between the people of the two sections there was continuous communication. Slaveholders came into
free States to liberate their slaves. Non-slaveholders came to get rid of the competition of slave
labor, and free negroes came to avoid reënslavement. Slaves fled thither on their way to liberty.
It was not a matter of choice; it was an unavoid-
able condition which compelled the people of the

border States to give continuous attention to the institution of slavery.

The modern anti-slavery movement had its origin in this great middle section, and from the same source it derived its chief support. The great body of active abolitionists were from the slave States or else derived their inspiration from personal contact with slavery. As compared with New England abolitionists, the middle-state folk were less extreme in their views. They had a keener appreciation of the difficulties involved in emancipation. They were more tolerant towards the idea of letting the country at large share the burdens involved in the liberation of the slaves. Border-state abolitionists naturally favored the policy of gradual emancipation which had been followed in New York, New Jersey, and Pennsylvania. Abolitionists who continued to reside in the slave States were forced to recognize the fact that emancipation involved serious questions of race adjustment. From the border States came the colonization society, a characteristic institution, as well as compromise of every variety.

The southernmost section, including South Carolina, Georgia, and the Gulf States, was even more sharply defined in the attitude it assumed toward the anti-slavery movement. At no time did the cause of emancipation become formidable in this section. In all these States there was, of course, a large class of non-slaveholding whites, who were opposed to slavery and who realized that they were victims of an injurious system; but they had no effective organ for expression. The ruling minority gained an early and an easy victory and to the end held a firm hand. To the inhabitants of this section it appeared to be a self-evident truth that the white race was born to rule and the black race was born to serve. Where negroes outnumbered the whites fourfold, the mere suggestion of emancipation raised a race question which seemed appalling in its proportions. Either in the Union or out of the Union, the rulers were determined to perpetuate slavery.

Slavery as an economic institution became dependent upon a few semitropical plantation crops. When the Constitution was framed, rice and indigo, produced in South Carolina and Georgia, were the two most important. Indigo declined in relative importance, and the production of sugar was developed, especially after the annexation of the Louisiana Purchase. But by far the most important crop for its effects upon slavery and upon the entire country was cotton. This single product finally absorbed the labor of half the slaves of the entire country. Mr. Rhodes is not at all unreasonable in his surmise that, had it not been for the unforeseen development of the cotton industry, the expectation of the founders of the Republic that slavery would soon disappear would actually have been realized.

It was more difficult to carry out a policy of emancipation when slaves were quoted in the market at a thousand dollars than when the price was a few hundred dollars. All slave-owners felt richer; emancipation appeared to involve a greater sacrifice. Thus the cotton industry went far towards accounting for the changed attitude of the entire country on the subject of slavery. The North as well as the South became financially interested.

It was not generally perceived before it actually happened that the border States would take the place of Africa in furnishing the required supply of laborers for Southern plantations. The interstate slave-trade gave to the system a solidarity of interest which was new. All slave-owners became partakers of a common responsibility for the system as a whole. It was the newly developed trade quite as much as the system of slavery itself which furnished the ground for the later anti-slavery appeal. The consciousness of a common guilt for the sin of slavery grew with the increase of actual interstate relations.

The abolition of the African slave-trade was an act of the general Government. Congress passed the prohibitory statute in 1807, to go into effect in January, 1808. At no time, however, was the prohibition entirely effective, and a limited illegal trade continued until slavery was eventually abolished. This inefficiency of restraint furnished another point of attack for the abolitionists. Through efforts to suppress the African slave-trade, the entire country became conscious of a common responsibility. Before the Revolutionary War, Great Britain had been censured for forcing cheap slaves from Africa upon her unwilling colonies. After the Revolution, New England was blamed for the activity of her citizens in this nefarious trade both before and after it was made illegal. All of this tended to increase the sense of responsibility in every section of the country. Congress had made the foreign slave-trade illegal; and citizens in all sections gradually became aware of the possibility that Congress might likewise restrict or forbid interstate commerce in slaves.

The West Indies and Mexico were also closely associated with the United States in the matter of slavery. When Jamestown was founded, negro slavery was already an old institution in the islands of the Caribbean Sea, and thence came the first slaves to Virginia. The abolition of slavery in the island of Hayti, or San Domingo, was accomplished during the French Revolution and the Napoleonic Wars. As incidental to the process of emancipation, the Caucasian inhabitants were massacred or banished, and a republican government was established, composed exclusively of negroes and mulattoes. From the date of the Missouri Compromise to that of the Mexican War, this island was united under a single republic, though it was afterwards divided into the two republics of Hayti and San Domingo.

The "horrors of San Domingo" were never absent from the minds of those in the United States who lived in communities composed chiefly of slaves. What had happened on the island was accepted by Southern planters as proof that the two races could live together in peace only under the relation of master and slave, and that emancipation boded the extermination of one race or the other. Abolitionists, however, interpreted the facts differently: they emphasized the tyranny of the white rulers as a primary cause of the massacres; they endowed some of the negro leaders with the highest qualities of statesmanship and self-sacrificing generosity; and Wendell Phillips, in an impassioned address which he delivered in 1861, placed on the honor roll above the chief worthies of history — including Cromwell and Washington — Toussaint L'Ouverture, the liberator of Hayti, whom France had betrayed and murdered.

Abolitionists found support for their position in the contention that other communities had abolished slavery without such accompanying horrors as occurred in Hayti and without serious race conflict. Slavery had run its course in Spanish America, and emancipation accompanied or followed the formation of independent republics. In 1833 all slaves in the British Empire were liberated, including those in the important island of Jamaica. So it happened that, just at the time when Southern leaders were making up their minds to defend their peculiar institution at all hazards, they were beset on every side by the spirit of emancipation. Abolitionists, on the other hand, were fully convinced that the attainment of some form of emancipation in the United States was certain, and that, either peaceably or through violence, the slaves would ultimately be liberated.

CHAPTER III

EARLY CRUSADERS

At the time when the new cotton industry was
enhancing the value of slave labor, there arose from
the ranks of the people those who freely consecrated their all to the freeing of the slave. Among
these, Benjamin Lundy, a New Jersey Quaker,
holds a significant place.

Though the Society of Friends fills a large place
in the anti-slavery movement, its contribution to
the growth of the conception of equality is even
more significant. This impetus to the idea arises
from a fundamental Quaker doctrine, announced
at the middle of the seventeenth century, to the
effect that God reveals Himself to mankind, not
through any priesthood or specially chosen agents;
not through any ordinance, form, or ceremony; not
through any church or institution; not through any
book or written record of any sort; but directly,
through His Spirit, to each person. This direct

enlightening agency they deemed coextensive with humanity; no race and no individual is left without the ever-present illuminating Spirit. If men of old spoke as they were moved by the Holy Spirit, what they spoke or wrote can furnish no reliable guidance to the men of a later generation, except as their minds also are enlightened by the same Spirit in the same way. "The letter killeth; it is the Spirit that giveth life."

This doctrine in its purity and simplicity places all men and all races on an equality; all are alike ignorant and imperfect; all are alike in their need of the more perfect revelation yet to be made. Master and slave are equal before God; there can be no such relation, therefore, except by doing violence to a personality, to a spiritual being. In harmony with this fundamental principle, the Society of Friends early rid itself of all connection with slavery. The Friends' Meeting became a refuge for those who were moved by the Spirit to testify against slavery.

Born in 1789 in a State which was then undergoing the process of emancipating its slaves, Benjamin Lundy moved at the age of nineteen to Wheeling, West Virginia, which had already become the center of an active domestic slave-trade. The pious young Quaker, now apprenticed to a saddler, was brought into personal contact with this traffic in human flesh. He felt keenly the national disgrace of the iniquity. So deep did the iron enter into his soul that never again did he find peace of mind except in efforts to relieve the oppressed. Like hundreds and thousands of others, Lundy was led on to active opposition to the trade by an actual knowledge of the inhumanity of the business as prosecuted before his eyes and by his sympathy for human suffering.

His apprenticeship ended, Lundy was soon established in a prosperous business in an Ohio village not far from Wheeling. Though he now lived in a free State, the call of the oppressed was ever in his ears and he could not rest. He drew together a few of his neighbors, and together they organized the Union Humane Society, whose object was the relief of those held in bondage. In a few months the society numbered several hundred members, and Lundy issued an address to the philanthropists of the whole country, urging them to unite in like manner with uniform constitutions, and suggesting that societies so formed adopt a policy of correspondence and coöperation. At about the same time, Lundy began to publish anti-slavery articles in the Mount Pleasant *Philanthropist* and other papers.

In 1819 he went on a business errand to St. Louis, Missouri, where he found himself in the midst of an agitation over the question of the extension of slavery in the States. With great zest he threw himself into the discussion, making use of the newspapers in Missouri and Illinois. Having lost his property, he returned poverty-stricken to Ohio, where he founded in January, 1821, the *Genius of Universal Emancipation*. A few months later he transferred his paper to the more congenial atmosphere of Jonesborough, Tennessee, but in 1824 he went to Baltimore, Maryland. In the meantime, Lundy had become much occupied in traveling, lecturing, and organizing societies for the promotion of the cause of abolition. He states that during the ten years previous to 1830 he had traveled upwards of twenty-five thousand miles, five thousand of which were on foot. He now became interested in plans for colonizing negroes in other countries as an aid to emancipation, though he himself had no confidence in the colonization society and its scheme of deportation to Africa. After leading a few negroes to Hayti in

1829, he visited Canada, Texas, and Mexico with a similar plan in view.

During a trip through the Middle States and New England in 1828, Lundy met William Lloyd Garrison, and the following year he walked all the way from Baltimore to Bennington, Vermont, for the express purpose of securing the assistance of the youthful reformer as coeditor of his paper. Garrison had previously favored colonization, but within the few weeks which elapsed before he joined Lundy, he repudiated all forms of colonization and advocated immediate and unconditional emancipation. He at once told Lundy of his change of views. "Well," said Lundy, "thee may put thy initials to thy articles, and I will put my witness to mine, and each will bear his own burden." The two editors were, however, in complete accord in their opposition to the slave-trade. Lundy had suffered a dangerous assault at the hands of a Baltimore slave-trader before he was joined by Garrison. During the year 1830, Garrison was convicted of libel and thrown into prison on account of his scathing denunciation of Francis Todd of Massachusetts, the owner of a vessel engaged in the slave-trade.

These events brought to a crisis the publication

of the *Genius of Universal Emancipation*.   The editors now parted company.   Again Lundy moved the office of the paper, this time to Washington. D. C., but it soon became a peripatetic monthly, printed wherever the editor chanced to be.   In 1836 Lundy began the issue of an anti-slavery paper in Philadelphia, called the *National Inquirer*, and with this was merged the *Genius of Universal Emancipation*.   He was preparing to resume the issue of his original paper under the old title, in La Salle County, Illinois, when he was overtaken by death on August 22, 1839.

Here was a man without education, without wealth, of a slight frame, not at all robust, who had undertaken, singlehanded and without the shadow of a doubt of his ultimate success, to abolish American slavery.   He began the organization of societies which were to displace the anti-slavery societies of the previous century.   He established the first paper devoted exclusively to the cause of emancipation.   He foresaw that the question of emancipation must be carried into politics and that it must become an object of concern to the general Government as well as to the separate States.   In the early part of his career he found the most congenial association and the larger measure of effective support south of Mason and Dixon's Line, and in this section were the greater number of the abolition societies which he organized. During the later years of his life, as it was becoming increasingly difficult in the South to maintain a public anti-slavery propaganda, he transferred his chief activities to the North. Lundy serves as a connecting link between the earlier and the later anti-slavery movements. Eleven years of his early life belong to the century of the Revolution. Garrison recorded his indebtedness to Lundy in the words: "If I have in any way, however humble, done anything towards calling attention to slavery, or bringing out the glorious prospect of a complete jubilee in our country at no distant day, I feel that I owe everything in this matter, instrumentally under God, to Benjamin Lundy."

Different in type, yet even more significant on account of its peculiar relations to the cause of abolition, was the life of James Gillespie Birney, who was born in a wealthy slaveholding family at Dansville, Kentucky, in the year 1792. The Birneys were anti-slavery planters of the type of Washington and Jefferson. The father had labored to make Kentucky a free State at the time of its admission to the Union. His son was educated

2

first at Princeton, where he graduated in 1810, and
then in the office of a distinguished lawyer in Philadelphia. He began the practice of law at his home
at the age of twenty-two. His home training and
his residence in States which were then in the process of gradual emancipation served to confirm him
in the traditional conviction of his family. While
Benjamin Lundy, at the age of twenty-seven, was
engaged in organizing anti-slavery societies north
of the Ohio River, Birney at the age of twenty-four
was influential as a member of the Kentucky Legislature in the prevention of the passing of a joint
resolution calling upon Ohio and Indiana to make
laws providing for the return of fugitive slaves.
He was also conspicuous in his efforts to secure
provisions for gradual emancipation. Two years
later he became a planter near Huntsville, Alabama. Though not a member of the Constitutional Convention preparatory to the admission
of this Territory into the Union, Birney used his
influence to secure provisions in the constitution
favorable to gradual emancipation. As a member
of the first Legislature, in 1819, he was the author
of a law providing a fair trial by jury for slaves
indicted for crimes above petty larceny, and in 1826
he became a regular contributor to the American

Colonization Society, believing it to be an aid to emancipation. The following year he was able to induce the Legislature, although he was not then a member of it, to pass an act forbidding the importation of slaves into Alabama either for sale or for hire. This was regarded as a step preliminary to emancipation.

The cause of education in Alabama had in Birney a trusted leader. During the year 1830 he spent several months in the North Atlantic States for the selection of a president and four professors for the State University and three teachers for the Huntsville Female Seminary. These were all employed upon his sole recommendation. On his return he had an important interview with Henry Clay, of whose political party he had for several years been the acknowledged leader in Alabama. He urged Clay to place himself at the head of the movement in Kentucky for gradual emancipation. Upon Clay's refusal their political coöperation terminated. Birney never again supported Clay for office and regarded him as in a large measure responsible for the pro-slavery reaction in Kentucky.

Birney, who had now become discouraged regarding the prospect of emancipation, during the winter of 1831 and 1832 decided to remove his

family to Jacksonville, Illinois. He was deterred
from carrying out his plan, however, by his unexpected appointment as agent of the colonization society in the Southwest — a mission which
he undertook from a sense of duty.

In his travels throughout the region assigned to
him, Birney became aware of the aggressive de-
signs of the planters of the Gulf States to secure
new slave territories in the Southwest. In view of
these facts the methods of the colonization society
appeared utterly futile. Birney surrendered his
commission and, in 1833, returned to Kentucky
with the intention of doing himself what Henry
Clay had refused to do three years earlier, still
hoping that Kentucky, Virginia, and Tennessee
might be induced to abolish slavery and thus place
the slave power in a hopeless minority. His dis-
appointment was extreme at the pro-slavery reaction which had taken place in Kentucky. The
condition called for more drastic measures, and
Birney decided to forsake entirely the colonization society and cast in his lot with the abolitionists. He freed his slaves in 1834, and in the following year he delivered the principal address at the
annual meeting of the American Anti-Slavery
Society held in New York. His gift of leadership

was at once recognized. As vice-president of the
society he began to travel on its behalf, to address
public assemblies, and especially to confer with
members of state legislatures and to address the
legislative bodies. He now devoted his entire
time to the service of the society, and as early as
September, 1835, issued the prospectus of a paper
devoted to the cause of emancipation. This called
forth such a display of force against the movement
that he could neither find a printer nor obtain the
use of a building in Dansville, Kentucky, for the
publication. As a result he transferred his activities to Cincinnati, where he began publication of
the *Philanthropist* in 1836. With the connivance
of the authorities and encouragement from leading
citizens of Cincinnati, the office of the *Philanthropist* was three times looted by the mob, and the
proprietor's life was greatly endangered. The
paper, however, rapidly grew in favor and influence
and thoroughly vindicated the right of free discussion of the slavery question. Another editor
was installed when Birney, who became secretary
of the Anti-Slavery Society in 1837, transferred
his residence to New York City.

Twenty-three years before Lincoln's famous
utterance in which he proclaimed the doctrine that

a house divided against itself cannot stand, and before Seward's declaration of an irrepressible conflict between slavery and freedom, Birney had said: "There will be no cessation of conflict until slavery shall be exterminated or liberty destroyed. Liberty and slavery cannot live in juxtaposition." He spoke out of the fullness of his own experience. A thoroughly trained lawyer and statesman, well acquainted with the trend of public sentiment in both North and South, he was fully persuaded that the new pro-slavery crusade against liberty boded civil war. He knew that the white men in North and South would not, without a struggle, consent to be permanently deprived of their liberties at the behest of a few Southern planters. Being himself of the slaveholding class, he was peculiarly fitted to appreciate their position. To him the new issue meant war, unless the belligerent leaders should be shown that war was hopeless. By his moderation in speech, his candor in statement, his lack of rancor, his carefully considered, thoroughly fair arguments, he had the rare faculty of convincing opponents of the correctness of his own view.

There could be little sympathy between Birney and William Lloyd Garrison, whose style of denunciation appeared to the former as an incitement to war and an excuse for mob violence. As soon as Birney became the accepted leader in the national society, there was friction between his followers and those of Garrison. To denounce the Constitution and repudiate political action were, from Birney's standpoint, a surrender of the only hope of forestalling a dire calamity. He had always fought slavery by the use of legal and constitutional methods, and he continued so to fight. In this policy he had the support of a large majority of abolitionists in New England and elsewhere. Only a few personal friends accepted Garrison's injunction to forswear politics and repudiate the Constitution.

The followers of Birney, failing to secure recognition for their views in either of the political parties, organized the Liberty party and, while Birney was in Europe in 1840, nominated him as their candidate for the Presidency. The vote which he received was a little over seven thousand, but four years later he was again the candidate of the party and received over sixty thousand votes. He suffered an injury during the following year which condemned him to hopeless invalidism and brought his public career to an end.

Though Lundy and Birney were contemporaries

and were engaged in the same great cause, they
were wholly independent in their work. Lundy
addressed himself almost entirely to the non-slaveholding class, while all of Birney's early efforts
were those of a slaveholder seeking to induce his
own class to support the policy of emancipation.
Though a Northern man, Lundy found his chief
support in the South until he was driven out by
persecution. Birney also resided in the South until
he was forced to leave for the same reason. The
two men were in general accord in their main lines
of policy: both believed firmly in the use of political
means to effect their objects; both were at first
colonizationists, though Lundy favored colonization in adjacent territory rather than by deportation to Africa.

Women were not a whit behind men in their
devotion to the cause of freedom. Conspicuous
among them were Sarah and Angelina Grimké,
born in Charleston, South Carolina, of a slaveholding family noted for learning, refinement, and cul-
ture. Sarah was born in the same year as James
G. Birney, 1792; Angelina was thirteen years
younger. Angelina was the typical crusader: her
sympathies from the first were with the slave. As

a child she collected and concealed oil and other simple remedies so that she might steal out by night and alleviate the sufferings of slaves who had been cruelly whipped or abused. At the age of fourteen she refused to be confirmed in the Episcopal Church because the ceremony involved giving sanction to words which seemed to her untrue. Two years later her mother offered her a present of a slave girl for a servant and companion. This gift she refused to accept, for in her view the servant had a right to be free, and, as for her own needs, Angelina felt quite capable of waiting upon herself.

Of her own free will she joined the Presbyterian Church and labored earnestly with the officers of the church to induce them to espouse the cause of the slave. When she failed to secure coöperation, she decided that the church was not Christian and she therefore withdrew her membership. Her sister Sarah had gone North in 1821 and had become a member of the Society of Friends in Philadelphia. In Charleston, South Carolina, there was a Friends' meeting-house where two old Quakers still met at the appointed time and sat for an hour in solemn silence. Angelina donned the Quaker garb, joined this meeting, and for an entire year was the third of the silent worshipers. This quiet testimony, however, did not wholly satisfy her energetic nature, and when, in 1830, she heard of the imprisonment of Garrison in Baltimore, she was convinced that effective labors against slavery could not be carried on in the South. With great sorrow she determined to sever her connection with home and family and join her sister in Philadelphia. There the exile from the South poured out her soul in an *Appeal to the Christian Women of the South*. The manuscript was handed to the officers of the Anti-Slavery Society in the city and, as they read, tears filled their eyes. The *Appeal* was immediately printed in large quantities for distribution in Southern States.

Copies of the *Appeal* which had been sent to Charleston were seized by a mob and publicly burned. When it became known soon afterwards that the author of the offensive document was intending to return to Charleston to spend the winter with her family, there was intense excitement, and the mayor of the city informed the mother that her daughter would not be permitted to land in Charleston nor to communicate with any one there, and that, if she did elude the police and come ashore, she would be imprisoned and guarded until the departure of the next boat. On account of the distress which she would cause to her friends, Miss Grimké reluctantly gave up the exercise of her constitutional right to visit her native city and in a very literal sense she became a permanent exile.

The two sisters let their light shine among Philadelphia Quakers. In the religious meetings negro women were consigned to a special seat. The Grimkés, having first protested against this discrimination, took their own places on the seat with the colored women. In Charleston, Angelina had scrupulously adhered to the Quaker garb because it was viewed as a protest against slavery. In Philadelphia, however, no such meaning was attached to the costume, and she adopted clothing suited to the climate regardless of conventions. A series of parlor talks to women which had been organized by the sisters grew in interest until the parlors became inadequate, and the speakers were at last addressing large audiences of women in the public meeting-places of Philadelphia.

At this time when Angelina was making effective use of her unrivaled power as a public speaker, she received in 1836 an invitation from the Anti-Slavery Society of New York to address the women of that city. She informed her sister that she

believed this to be a call from God and that it was
her duty to accept. Sarah decided to be her companion and assistant in the work in the new field,
which was similar to that in Philadelphia. Its
fame soon extended to Boston, whence came an
urgent invitation to visit that city. It was in
Massachusetts that men began to steal into the
women's meetings and listen from the back seats.
In Lynn all barriers were broken down, and a
modest, refined, and naturally diffident young
woman found herself addressing immense audiences of men and women. In the old theater in
Boston for six nights in succession, audiences filling
all the space listened entranced to the messenger
of emancipation. There is uniform testimony
that, in an age distinguished for oratory, no more
effective speaker appeared than Angelina Grimké.
It was she above all others who first vindicated the
right of women to speak to men from the public
platform on political topics. But it must be remembered that scores of other women were laboring to the same end and were fully prepared to
utilize the new opportunity.

The great world movement from slavery towards
freedom, from despotism to democracy, is characterized by a tendency towards the equality of the

sexes. Women have been slaves where men were free. In barbarous ages women have been ignored or have been treated as mere adjuncts to the ruling sex. But wherever there has been a distinct contribution to the cause of liberty there has been a distinct recognition of woman's share in the work. The Society of Friends was organized on the principle that men and women are alike moral beings, hence are equal in the sight of God. As a matter of experience, women were quite as often moved to break the silence of a religious meeting as were the men.

For two hundred years women had been accustomed to talk to both men and women in Friends' meetings and, when the moral war against slavery brought religion and politics into close relation, they were ready speakers upon both topics. When the Grimké sisters came into the church with a fresh baptism of the Spirit, they overcame all obstacles and, with a passion for righteousness, moral and spiritual and political, they carried the war against slavery into politics.

In 1833, at the organization of the American Anti-Slavery Society in Philadelphia, a number of women were present. Lucretia Mott, a distinguished "minister" in the Society of Friends, took part in the proceedings. She was careful to state that she spoke as a mere visitor, having no place in the organization, but she ventured to suggest various modifications in the report of Garrison's committee on a declaration of principles which rendered it more acceptable to the meeting. It had not then been seriously considered whether women could become members of the Anti-Slavery Society, which was at that time composed exclusively of men, with the women maintaining their separate organizations as auxiliaries.

The women of the West were already better organized than the men and were doing a work which men could not do. They were, for the most part, unconscious of any conflict between the peculiar duties of men and those of women in their relations to common objects. The "library associations" of Indiana, which were in fact effective anti-slavery societies, were to a large extent composed of women. To the library were added numerous other disguises, such as "reading circles," "sewing societies," "women's clubs." In many communities the appearance of men in any of these enterprises would create suspicion or even raise a mob. But the women worked on quietly, effectively, and unnoticed.

The matron of a family would be provided with the best riding-horse which the neighborhood could furnish. Mounted upon her steed, she would sally forth in the morning, meet her carefully selected friends in a town twenty miles away, gain information as to what had been accomplished, give information as to the work in other parts of the district, distribute new literature, confer as to the best means of extending their labors, and return in the afternoon. The father of such a family was quite content with the humbler task of coöperation by supplying the sinews of war. There was complete equality between husband and wife because their aims were identical and each rendered the service most convenient and most needed. Women did what men could not do. In the territory of the enemy the men were reached through the gradual and tentative efforts of women whom the uninitiated supposed to be spending idle hours at a sewing circle. Interest was maintained by the use of information of the same general character as that which later took the country by storm in *Uncle Tom's Cabin*. In course of time all disguise was thrown aside. A public speaker of national reputation would appear, a meeting would be announced, and a rousing abolition speech would be delivered; the mere men of the neighborhood would have little conception how the surprising change had been accomplished.

On rare occasions the public presentation of the anti-slavery view would be undertaken prematurely, as in 1840 at Pendleton, Indiana, when Frederick Douglass attempted to address a public meeting and was almost slain by missiles from the mob. Pendleton, however, was not given over to the enemy. The victim of the assault was restored to health in the family of a leading citizen. The outrage was judiciously utilized to convince the fair-minded that one of the evils of slavery was the development of minds void of candor and justice. On the twenty-fifth anniversary of the Pendleton disturbance there was another great meeting in the town. Frederick Douglass was the hero of the occasion. The woman who was the head of the family that restored him to health was on the platform. Some of the men who threw the brickbats were there to make public confession and to apologize for the brutal deed.

In the minds of a few persons of rare intellectual and logical endowment, democracy has always implied the equality of the sexes. From the time of the French Revolution there have been advocates of this doctrine. As early as 1820, Frances Wright, a young woman in Scotland having knowledge of the Western republic founded upon the professed principles of liberty and equality, came to America for the express purpose of pleading the cause of equal rights for women. To the general public her doctrine seemed revolutionary, threatening the very foundations of religion and morality. In the midst of opposition and persecution she proclaimed views respecting the rights and duties of women which today are generally accepted as axiomatic.

The women who attended the meetings for the organization of the American Anti-Slavery Society were not suffragists, nor had they espoused any special theories respecting the position of women. They did not wish to be members of the men's organizations but were quite content with their own separate one, which served its purpose very well under prevailing local conditions. James G. Birney, the candidate of the Liberty party for the Presidency in 1840, had good reasons for opposition to the inclusion of men and women in the same organization. He knew that by acting separately they were winning their way. The introduction of a novel theory involving a different issue seemed to him likely to be a source of weakness.

The cause of women was, however, gaining ground and winning converts. Lucretia Mott and Elizabeth Cady Stanton were delegates to the World's Anti-Slavery Convention at London. They listened to the debate which ended in the refusal to recognize them as members of the Convention because they were women. The tone of the discussion convinced them that women were looked upon by men with disdain and contempt. Because the laws of the land and the customs of society consigned women to an inferior position, and because there would be no place for effective public work on the part of women until these laws were changed, both these women became advocates of women's rights and conspicuous leaders in the initiation of the propaganda. The Reverend Samuel J. May, of Syracuse, New York, preached a sermon in 1845 in which he stated his belief that women need not expect to have their wrongs fully redressed until they themselves had a hand in the making and in the administration of the laws. This is an early suggestion that equal suffrage would become the ultimate goal of the efforts for righting women's wrongs.

At the same time there were accessions to the cause from a different source. In 1833 Oberlin

College was founded in northern Ohio. Into some of the first classes there women were admitted on equal terms with men. In 1835 the trustees offered the presidency to Professor Asa Mahan, of Lane Seminary. He was himself an abolitionist from a slave State, and he refused to be President of Oberlin College unless negroes were admitted on equal terms with other students. Oberlin thus became the first institution in the country which extended the privileges of the higher education to both sexes of all races. It was a distinctly religious institution devoted to radical reforms of many kinds. Not only was the use of all intoxicating beverages discarded by faculty and students but the use of tobacco as well was discouraged.

Within fifteen years after the founding of Oberlin, there were women graduates who had something to say on numerous questions of public interest. Especially was this true of the subject of temperance. Intemperance was a vice peculiar to men. Women and children were the chief sufferers, while men were the chief sinners. It was important, therefore, that men should be reached. In 1847 Lucy Stone, an Oberlin graduate, began to address public audiences on the subject. At the same time Susan B. Anthony appeared as a temperance lecturer. The manner of their reception and the nature of their subject induced them to unite heartily in the pending crusade for the equal rights of women. The three causes thus became united in one.

Along with the crusade against slavery, intemperance, and women's wrongs, arose a fourth, which was fundamentally connected with the slavery question. Quakers and Southern and Western abolitionists were ardently devoted to the interests of peace. They would abolish slavery by peaceable means because they believed the alternative was a terrible war. To escape an impending war they were nerved to do and dare and to incur great risks. New England abolitionists who labored in harmony with those of the West and South were actuated by similar motives. Sumner first gained public notice by a distinguished oration against war. Garrison went farther: he was a professional non-resistant, a root and branch opponent of both war and slavery. John Brown was a fanatical antagonist of war until he reached the conclusion that according to the Divine Will there should be a short war of liberation in place of the continuance of slavery, which was itself in his opinion the most cruel form of war.

Slavery as a legally recognized institution disappeared with the Civil War. The war against intemperance has made continuous progress and this problem is apparently approaching a solution. The war against war as a recognized institution has become the one all-absorbing problem of civilization. The war against the wrongs of women is being supplanted by efforts to harmonize the mutual privileges and duties of men and women on the basis of complete equality. As Samuel May predicted more than seventy years ago, in the future women are certain to take a hand both in the making and in the administration of law.

CHAPTER IV

THE TURNING-POINT

THE year 1831 is notable for three events in the history of the anti-slavery controversy: on the first day of January in that year William Lloyd Garrison began in Boston the publication of the *Liberator;* in August there occurred in Southampton, Virginia, an insurrection of slaves led by a negro, Nat Turner, in which sixty-one white persons were massacred; and in December the Virginia Legislature began its long debate on the question of slavery.

On the part of the abolitionists there was at no time any sudden break in the principles which they advocated. Lundy did nothing but revive and continue the work of the Quakers and other non slaveholding classes of the revolutionary period. Birney was and continued to be a typical slave holding abolitionist of the earlier period. Garrison began his work as a disciple of Lundy, whom

he followed in the condemnation of the African
colonization scheme, though he went farther and
rejected every form of colonization. Garrison likewise repudiated every plan for gradual emancipation and proclaimed the duty of immediate and
unconditional liberation of the slaves.

The first number of the *Liberator* contained an
Address to the Public, which sounded the key-
note of Garrison's career. "I shall contend for the
immediate enfranchisement of our slave population — I will be as harsh as truth and as uncompromising as justice on this subject — I do not
wish to think, or speak, or write with moderation
— I am in earnest — I will not equivocate — I
will not retreat a single inch, and *I will be heard!*"

The New England Anti-Slavery Society, of
which Garrison was the chief organizer, was in
essential harmony with the societies which Lundy
had organized in other sections. Its first address
to the public in 1833 distinctly recognized the
separate States as the sole authority in the matter of emancipation within their own boundaries.
Through moral suasion, eschewing all violence and
sedition, its authors proposed to secure their object. In the spirit of civil and religious liberty and
by appealing to the Declaration of Independence,

to the spirit and letter of the Constitution, they ex-
horted the entire people to become an effective anti-
slavery society. At the organization of the American Anti-Slavery Society a year later, the division
of power between the separate States and the
general Government, which found final expression
in the platform of the Republican party in 1856,
was recognized in its constitution, and in a declaration of principles written by Garrison himself
occur the words: "We also maintain that there are,
at the present time, the highest obligations resting
upon the people of the free States to remove slavery
by moral and political action, as prescribed in the
Constitution of the United States."   All the abolitionists were united on the main lines of policy
In 1835 Garrison, in the *Liberator*, called God to
witness that "we are not hostile to the Constitution of the United States."   It was many year
before Garrison applied to the cause of abolition
the peculiar doctrine of non-resistance and philo-
sophic anarchy in such a way as to separate himsel
and his few followers from the great body of abolitionists. Not until 1843 did he place at the hea
of his paper the words: "The compact which exist
between the North and the South is a covenan
with death and an agreement with Hell — involv

ing both parties in atrocious criminality and should be immediately annulled." Eleven years later he publicly burned a copy of the Constitution in the streets of Boston, crying aloud, "So perish all compromisers with tyranny."

In the meantime a division had arisen among New England abolitionists, and at the annual meeting of the national society in New York in 1840 the opponents of Garrison withdrew and organized the American and "Foreign" Anti-Slavery Society. The disagreement arose partly from a dispute over the question of the admission of women to membership, but chiefly because of Garrison's changing attitude towards participation in politics. Garrison's branch retained the old name and was designated as the "Old Society." It was in fact, however, a brand-new society proclaiming doctrines and advocating policies in direct contradiction to those of the original organization. Probably not one in a hundred of even the New England abolitionists ever accepted the special views which the Garrisonian organization adopted after 1843.

The facts that Garrison himself had a leading part in formulating the principles and policies for political action which received new emphasis by

the Liberty party of 1840 and 1844, by the Free-
soil party of 1848, and later by the Republican
party, and that nearly all of the abolitionists continued to be faithful adherents to those principles,
are sufficient proof of the essential unity of the
great anti-slavery movement. The apparent lack
of harmony and the real confusion in the history of
the subject arose from the peculiar character of one
remarkable man.

The few owners of slaves who had assumed the
rôle of public defenders of the institution were in
the habit of using violent and abusive language
against anti-slavery agitators. This appeared in
the first debate on the subject during Washington's
administration. Every form of rhetorical abuse
also accompanied the outbreak of mob violence
against the reformers at the time of Garrison's
advent into the controversy. He was especially
fitted to reply in kind. "I am accused," said he,
"of using hard language. I admit the charge. I
have not been able to find a soft word to describe
villainy, or to identify the perpetrator of it." This
was a new departure which was instantly recognized by Southern leaders. But from the beginning to the bitter end, Garrison stands alone as
preëminently the representative of this form of

attack.   It was significant, also, that the *Liberator*
was published in Boston, the literary center of the
country.

There is no evidence that there was any direct
connection between the publication of the *Liberator*
and the servile insurrection which occurred during the following August.[1]   It was, however, but
natural that the South should associate the two
events.   A few utterances of the paper were fitted,
if not intended, to incite insurrection.   One passage
reads: "Whenever there is a contest between the
oppressed and the oppressor — the weapons being
equal between the parties — God knows that my
heart must be with the oppressed, and always
against the oppressor.   Therefore, whenever com-
menced, I cannot but wish success to all slave insurrections."   Again: "Rather than see men wear-
ing their chains in a cowardly and servile spirit, I
would, as an advocate of peace, much rather see
them breaking the heads of the tyrant with their
chains."

George Thompson, an English colaborer with

[1] Garrison himself denied any direct connection with the Nat
Turner insurrection.   See *William Lloyd Garrison, the Story of His
Life told by His Children*, vol. i, p. 251.

Garrison, is quoted as saying in a public address in 1835 that "Southern slaves ought, or at least had a right, to cut the throats of their masters."[1] Such utterances are rare, and they express a passing mood not in the least characteristic of the general spirit of the abolition movement; yet the fact that such statements did emanate from such a source made it comparatively easy for extremists of the opposition to cast odium upon all abolitionists. The only type of abolition known in South Carolina was that of the extreme Garrisonian agitators, and it furnished at least a shadow of excuse for mob violence in the North and for complete suppression of discussion in the South. To encourage slaves to cut the throats of their masters was far from being a rhetorical figure of speech in communities where slaves were in the majority. Santo Domingo was at the time a prosperous republic founded by former slaves who had exterminated the Caucasian residents of the island. Negroes from Santo Domingo had fomented insurrection in South Carolina. The Nat Turner incident was more than a suggestion of the dire possibilities of the situation. Turner was a trusted slave, a

[1] Schouler, *History of the United States under the Constitution*, vol. v, p. 217.

preacher among the blacks. He succeeded in concealing his plot for weeks. When the massacre
began, slaves not in the secret were induced to
join. A majority of the slain were women and children. Abolitionists who had lived in slave States
never indulged in flippant remarks fitted to incite
insurrection. This was reserved for the few agitators far removed from the scene of action.

Southern planters who had determined at all
hazards to perpetuate the institution of slavery
were peculiarly sensitive on account of what was
taking place in Spanish America and in the British
West Indies. Mexico abolished slavery in 1829,
and united with Colombia in encouraging Cuba
to throw off the Spanish yoke, abolish slavery, and
join the sisterhood of New World republics. This
led to an effective protest on the part of the United
States. Both Spain and Mexico were advised that
the United States could not with safety to its own
interests permit the emancipation of slaves in the
island of Cuba. But with the British Emancipation Act of 1833, Cuba became the only neighboring
territory in which slavery was legal. These acts of
emancipation added zeal to the determination of
the Southern planters to secure territory for the
indefinite extension of slavery to the southwest.

When Lundy and Birney discovered these plans, their desire to husband and extend the direct political influence of abolitionists was greatly stimulated.   To this end they maintained a moderate and conservative attitude.   They took care that no abuse or misrepresentation should betray them into any expression which would diminish their influence with fair-minded, reasonable men. They were convinced that a clear and complete revelation of the facts would lead a majority of the people to adopt their views.

The debate in the Virginia Legislature in the session which met three months after the Southampton massacre furnishes a demonstration that the traditional anti-slavery sentiment still persisted among the rulers of the Old Dominion.   It arose out of a petition from the Quakers of the State asking for an investigation preparatory to a gradual emancipation of the slaves.   The debate, which lasted for several weeks, was able and thorough. No stronger utterances in condemnation of slavery were ever voiced than appear in this debate. Different speakers made the statement that no one presumed to defend slavery on principle — that apologists for slavery existed but no defenders.

Opposition to the petition was in the main apologetic in tone.

A darker picture of the blighting effects of slavery on the industries of the country was never drawn than appears in these speeches. Slavery was declared to be driving free laborers from the State, to have already destroyed every industry except agriculture, and to have exhausted the soil so that profitable agriculture was becoming extinct, while pine brush was encroaching upon former fruitful fields. "Even the wolf," said one, "driven back long since by the approach of man, now returns, after the lapse of a hundred years, to howl over the desolations of slavery." Contrasts between free labor in northern industry and that of the South were vividly portrayed. In a speech of great power, one member referred to Kentucky and Ohio as States "providentially designated to exhibit in their future histories the differences which necessarily result from a country free from, and a country afflicted with the curse of slavery."

The debate was by no means confined to industrial or material considerations. McDowell, who was afterwards elected Governor of the State, thus portrays the personal relations of master and slave: "You may place the slave where you please — you

may put him under any process, which, without
destroying his value as a slave, will debase and
crush him as a rational being — you may do all this,
and the idea that he was born to be free will sur-
vive it all. It is allied to his hope of immortality —
it is the ethereal part of his nature which oppres-
sion cannot reach — it is a torch lit up in his soul
by the hand of the Deity, and never meant to be
extinguished by the hand of man."

Various speakers assumed that the continuance
of slavery involved a bloody conflict; that either
peaceably or through violence, slavery as contrary
to the spirit of the age must come to an end; that
the agitation against it could not be suppressed.
Faulkner drew a lurid picture of the danger from
servile insurrection, in which he referred to the
utterances of two former speakers, one of whom
had said that, unless something effective was done
to ward off the danger, "the throats of all the white
people of Virginia will be cut." The other replied,
"No, the whites cannot be conquered — the
throats of the blacks will be cut." Faulkner's re-
joinder was that the difference was a trifling one,
"for the fact is conceded that one race or the other
must be exterminated."

The public press joined in the debate. Leading

editorials appeared in the *Richmond Enquirer* urging that effective measures be instituted to put an end to slavery. The debate aroused much interest throughout the South. Substantially all the current abolition arguments appeared in the speeches of the slave-owning members of the Virginia Legislature. And what was done about it? Nothing at all. The petition was not granted; no action looking towards emancipation was taken. This was indeed a turning-point. Men do not continue to denounce in public their own conduct unless their action results in some effort toward corrective measures.

Professor Thomas Dew, of the chair of history and metaphysics in William and Mary College and later President of the College, published an essay reviewing the debate in the Legislature and arguing that any plan for emancipation in Virginia was either undesirable or impossible. This essay was among the first of the direct pro-slavery arguments. Statements in support of the view soon followed. In 1835 the Governor of South Carolina in a message to the Legislature said, "Domestic slavery is the corner-stone of our republican edifice." Senator Calhoun, speaking in the Senate two years later, declared slavery to be a positive good.

W. G. Simms, Southern poet and novelist, writing
in 1852, felicitates himself as being among the first
who about fifteen years earlier advocated slavery
as a great good and a blessing. Harriet Martineau,
an English author who traveled extensively in the
South in 1835, found few slaveholders who justified
the institution as being in itself just. But after
the debates in the Virginia Legislature, there were
few owners of slaves who publicly advocated abolition. The spirit of mob violence had set in,
and, contrary to the utterances of Virginia statesmen, free speech on the subject of slavery was
suppressed in the slave States. This did not mean
that Southern statesmen had lost the power to per-
ceive the evil effects of slavery or that they were
convinced that their former views were erroneous.
It meant simply that they had failed to agree
upon a policy of gradual emancipation, and the
only recourse left seemed to be to follow the example of James G. Birney and leave the South or
to submit in silence to the new order.

CHAPTER V

WITH the changed attitude of the South towards emancipation there was associated an active hostility to dearly bought human liberty. Freedom of speech, freedom of the press, freedom of worship, the right of assembly, trial by jury, the right of petition, free use of the mails, and numerous other fundamental human rights were assailed. Birney and other abolitionists who had immediate knowledge of slavery early perceived that the real question at issue was quite as much the continued liberty of the white man as it was the liberation of the black man and that the enslavement of one race involved also the ultimate essential enslavement of the other.

In 1831 two slave States and six free States still extended to free negroes the right to vote. During the pro-slavery crusade these privileges disappeared; and not only so, but free negroes were banished from certain States, or were not permitted to enter them, or were allowed to remain only by choosing a white man for a guardian. It was made a crime to teach negroes, whether slaves or free men, to read and write. Under various pretexts free negroes were reduced to slavery. Freedom of worship was denied to negroes, and they were not allowed to assemble for any purpose except under the strict surveillance of white men. Negro testimony in a court of law was invalid where the rights of a white man were involved. The right of a negro to his freedom was decided by an arbitrary court without a jury, while the disputed right of a white man to the ownership of a horse was conditioned by the safeguard of trial by jury.

The maintenance of such policies carries with it of necessity the suppression of free discussion. When Southern leaders adopted the policy of defending slavery as a righteous institution, abolitionists in the South either emigrated to the North or were silenced. In either case they were deprived of a fundamental right. The spirit of persecution followed them into the free States. Birney could not publish his paper in Kentucky, nor even at Cincinnati, save at the risk of his life.

Elijah Lovejoy was not allowed to publish his
paper in Missouri, and, when he persisted in publishing it in Illinois, he was brutally murdered.
Even in Boston it required men of courage and determination to meet and organize an anti-slavery
society in 1832, though only a few years earlier
Benjamin Lundy had traveled freely through the
South itself delivering anti-slavery lectures and
organizing scores of such societies. The New York
Anti-Slavery Society was secretly organized in 1832
in spite of the opposition of a determined mob.
Mob violence was everywhere rife. Meetings
were broken up, negro quarters attacked, property
destroyed, murders committed.

Fair-minded men became abolitionists on account of the crusade against the rights of white
men quite as much as from their interest in the
rights of negroes. Salmon P. Chase of Ohio was
led to espouse the cause by observing the attacks
upon the freedom of the press in Cincinnati. Gerrit Smith witnessed the breaking up of an anti-
slavery meeting in Utica, New York, and thereafter consecrated his time, his talents, and his great
wealth to the cause of liberty. Wendell Phillips
saw Garrison in the hands of a Boston mob, and
that experience determined him to make common

cause with the martyr. And the murder of Lovejoy in 1837 made many active abolitionists.

It is difficult to imagine a more inoffensive practice than giving to negro girls the rudiments of an education. Yet a school for this purpose, taught by Miss Prudence Crandall in Canterbury, Connecticut, was broken up by persistent persecution, a special act of the Legislature being passed for the purpose, forbidding the teaching of negroes from outside the State without the consent of the town authorities. Under this act Miss Crandall was arrested, convicted, and imprisoned.

Having eliminated free discussion from the South, the Southern States sought to accomplish the same object in the North. In pursuance of a resolution of the Legislature, the Governor of Georgia offered a reward of five thousand dollars to any one who should arrest, bring to trial, and prosecute to conviction under the laws of Georgia the editor of the *Liberator*. R. G. Williams, publishing agent for the American Anti-Slavery Society, was indicted by a grand jury of Tuscaloosa County, Alabama, and Governor Gayle of Alabama made a requisition on Governor Marcy of New York for his extradition. Williams had never been in Alabama. His offense consisted in publishing in the

New York *Emancipator* a few rather mild utterances against slavery.

Governor McDuffie of South Carolina in an official message declared that slavery was the very corner-stone of the republic, adding that the laboring population of any country, "bleached or unbleached," was a dangerous element in the body politic, and predicting that within twenty-five years the laboring people of the North would be virtually reduced to slavery. Referring to abolitionists, he said: "The laws of every community should punish this species of interference with death without benefit of clergy." Pursuant to the Governor's recommendation, the Legislature adopted a resolution calling upon non-slaveholding States to pass laws to suppress promptly and effectively all abolition societies. In nearly all the slave States similar resolutions were adopted, and concerted action against anti-slavery effort was undertaken. During the winter of 1835 and 1836, the Governors of the free States received these resolutions from the South and, instead of resenting them as an uncalled-for interference with the rights of free commonwealths, they treated them with respect. Edward Everett, Governor of Massachusetts, in his message presenting the Southern documents to the Legislature, said: "Whatever by direct and necessary operation is calculated to excite an insurrection among the slaves has been held, by highly respectable legal authority, an offense against this Commonwealth which may be prosecuted as a misdemeanor at common law." Governor Marcy of New York, in a like document, declared that "without the power to pass such laws the States would not possess all the necessary means for preserving their external relations of peace among themselves." Even before the Southern requests reached Rhode Island, the Legislature had under consideration a bill to suppress abolition societies.

When a committee of the Massachusetts Legislature had been duly organized to consider the documents received from the slave States, the abolitionists requested the privilege of a hearing before the committee. Receiving no reply, they proceeded to formulate a statement of their case; but before they could publish it, they were invited to appear before the joint committee of the two houses. The public had been aroused by the issue and there was a large audience. The case for the abolitionists was stated by their ablest speakers, among whom was William Lloyd Garrison. They

labored to convince the committee that their utterances were not incendiary, and that any legislative
censure directed against them would be an encouragement to mob violence and the persecution
which was already their lot. After the defensive
arguments had been fully presented, William Goodell took the floor and proceeded to charge upon the
Southern States which had made these demands a
conspiracy against the liberties of the North. In
the midst of great excitement and many interrup-
tions by the chairman of the committee, he quoted
the language of Governor McDuffie's message,
and characterized the documents lying on the
table before him as "fetters for Northern freemen."
Then, turning to the committee, he began, "Mr.
Chairman, are you prepared to attempt to put
them on?" — but the sentence was only half
finished when the stentorian voice of the chairman
interrupted him: "Sit down, sir!" and he sat
down. The committee then arose and left the
room. But the audience did not rise; they wailed
till other abolitionists found their tongues and gave
expression to a fixed determination to uphold the
liberties purchased for them by the blood of their
fathers. The Massachusetts Legislature did not
comply with the request of Governor McDuffie of

South Carolina to take the first step towards the enslavement of all laborers, white as well as black. And Rhode Island refused to enact into law the pending bill for the suppression of anti-slavery societies. They declined to violate the plain requirements of their Constitution that the interests of slavery might be promoted. Not many years later they were ready to strain or break the Constitution for the sake of liberty.

In the general crusade against liberty churches proved more pliable than States. The authority of nearly all the leading denominations was directed against the abolitionists. The General Conference of the Methodist Episcopal Church passed in 1836 a resolution censuring two of their members who had lectured in favor of modern abolitionism. The Ohio Conference of the same denomination had passed resolutions urging resistance to the anti-slavery movement. In June, 1836, the New York Conference decided that no one should be chosen as deacon or elder who did not give pledge that he would refrain from agitating the church on the subject.

The same spirit appeared in theological seminaries. The trustees of Lane Seminary, near Cincinnati, Ohio, voted that students should not organize or be members of anti-slavery societies or hold meetings or lecture or speak on the subject. Whereupon the students left in a body, and many of the professors withdrew and united with others in the founding of an anti-slavery college at Oberlin.

A persistent attack was also directed against the use of the United States mails for the distribution of anti-slavery literature.   Mob violence which involved the post-office began as early as 1830, when printed copies of Miss Grimké's *Appeal to the Christian Women of the South* were seized and burned in Charleston.   In 1835 large quantities of anti-slavery literature were removed from the Charleston office and in the presence of the assembled citizens committed to the flames.   Postmasters on their own motion examined the mails and refused to deliver any matter that they deemed incendiary. Amos Kendall, Postmaster-General, was requested to issue an order authorizing such conduct.   He replied that he had no legal authority to issue such an order.   Yet he would not recommend the delivery of such papers.   "We owe," said he, "an obligation to the laws, but a higher one to the communities in which we live, and if the former be perverted to destroy the latter, it is patriotism to disregard them.   Entertaining these views, I cannot sanction, and will not condemn, the step you have taken." This is an early instance of the appeal to the "higher law" in the pro-slavery controversy. The higher law was invoked against the freedom of the press. The New York postmaster sought to dissuade the Anti-Slavery Society from the attempt to send its publications through the mails into Southern States. In reply to a request for authorization to refuse to accept such publications, the Postmaster-General replied: "I am deterred from giving an order to exclude the whole series of abolition publications from the Southern mails only by a want of legal power, and if I were situated as you are, I would do as you have done."

Mr. Kendall's letters to the postmasters of Charleston and New York were written in July and August, 1835. In December of the same year, presumably with full knowledge that a member of his Cabinet was encouraging violations of law in the interest of slavery, President Jackson undertook to supply the need of legal authorization. In his annual message he made a savage attack upon the abolitionists and recommended to Congress the "passing of such a law as will prohibit, under severe penalties, the circulation in the Southern

States, through the mail, of incendiary publications."

This part of the President's message was referred to a select committee, of which John C. Calhoun was chairman. The chairman's report was against the adoption of the President's recommendation because a subject of such vital interest to the States ought not to be left to Congress. The admission of the right of Congress to decide what is incendiary, asserted the report, carries with it the power to decide what is not incendiary and hence Congress might authorize and enforce the circulation of abolition literature through the mails in all the States. The States should themselves severally decide what in their judgment is incendiary, and then it would become the duty of the general Government to give effect to such state laws. The bill recommended was in harmony with this view. It was made illegal for any deputy postmaster "to deliver to any person whatsoever, any pamphlet, newspaper, handbill, or other printed paper, or pictorial representation touching the subject of slavery, where by the laws of the said State, territory, or district their circulation is prohibited." The bill was defeated in the Senate by a small margin. Altogether there was an enlightening

debate on the whole subject. The exposure of
the abuse of tampering with the mail created a
general reaction, which enabled the abolitionists
to win a spectacular victory. Instead of a law forbidding the circulation of anti-slavery publications,
Congress enacted a law requiring postal officials
under heavy penalties to deliver without discrimination all matter committed to their charge.
This act was signed by President Jackson, and Calhoun himself was induced to admit that the purposes of the abolitionists were not violent and
revolutionary. Henceforth abolitionists enjoyed
their full privileges in the use of the United States
mail.

An even more dramatic victory was thrust upon
the abolitionists by the inordinate violence of their
opponents in their attack upon the right of petition. John Quincy Adams, who became their
distinguished champion, was not himself an abolitionist. When, as a member of the lower House of
Congress in 1831, he presented petitions from certain citizens of Pennsylvania, presumably Quakers,
requesting Congress to abolish slavery and the
slave-trade in the District of Columbia, he refused
to countenance their prayer, and expressed the
wish that the memorial might be referred without

debate. At the very time when a New England ex-President was thus advising abolitionists to desist from sending petitions to Congress, the Virginia Legislature was engaged in the memorable debate upon a similar petition from Virginia Quakers, in which most radical abolition sentiment was expressed by actual slave-owners. Adams continued to present anti-slavery memorials and at the same time to express his opposition to the demands of the petitioners. When in 1835 there arose a decided opposition to the reception of such documents, Adams, still in apparent sympathy with the pro-slavery South on the main issue, gave wise counsel on the method of dealing with petitions. They should be received, said he, and referred to a committee; because the right of petition is sacred. This, he maintained, was the best way to avoid disturbing debate on the subject of slavery. He quoted his own previous experience; he had made known his opposition to the purposes of the petitioners; their memorials were duly referred to a committee and there they slept the sleep of death. At that time only one voice had been raised in the House in support of the abolition petitioners, that of John Dickson of New York, who had delivered a speech of two hours in length advocating their

cause; but not a voice was raised in reply. Mr.
Adams mentioned this incident with approval.
The way to forestall disturbing debate in Congress,
he said, was scrupulously to concede all constitutional rights and then simply to refrain from speaking on the subject.

This sound advice was not followed. For several
months a considerable part of the time of the House
was occupied with the question of handling abolition petitions. And finally, in May, 1836, the
following resolution passed the House: "*Resolved*,
That all petitions, memorials, resolutions, proposi-
tions, or papers relating in any way or to any
extent whatever to the subject of slavery or the
abolition of slavery, shall, without being either
printed or referred, be laid on the table, and that
no further action whatever shall be had thereon."
This is commonly known as the "gag resolution."
During four successive years it was reënacted in
one form or another and was not repealed by
direct vote until 1844.

When the name of Mr. Adams was called in the
vote upon the passage of the above resolution, instead of answering in the ordinary way, he said:
"I hold the resolution to be a direct violation of
the Constitution of the United States, of the rules

of this House, and of the rights of my constituents." This was the beginning of the duel between the "old man eloquent" and a determined majority in the House of Representatives. Adams developed undreamed-of resources as a debater and parliamentarian. He made it his special business to break down the barrier against the right of petition. Abolitionists coöperated with zeal in the effort. Their champion was abundantly supplied with petitions. The gag resolution was designed to prevent all debate on the subject of slavery. Its effect in the hands of the shrewd parliamentarian was to foment debate. On one occasion, with great apparent innocence, after presenting the usual abolition petitions, Adams called the attention of the Speaker to one which purported to be signed by twenty-two slaves and asked whether such a petition should be presented to the House, since he was himself in doubt as to the rules applicable in such a case. This led to a furious outbreak in the House which lasted for three days. Adams was threatened with censure at the bar of the House, with expulsion, with the grand jury, with the penitentiary; and it is believed that only his great age and national repute shielded him from personal violence. After numerous passionate speeches had been

delivered, Adams injected a few important correc-
tions into the debate. He reminded the House
that he had not presented a petition purporting
to emanate from slaves; on the contrary, he had
expressly declined to present it until the Speaker
had decided whether a petition from slaves was
covered by the rule. Moreover, the petition was
not against slavery but in favor of slavery. He
was then charged with the crime of trifling with the
sensibilities of the House; and finally the champion
of the right of petition took the floor in his own defense. His language cut to the quick. His calum-
niators were made to feel the force of his biting
sarcasm. They were convicted of injustice, and all
their resolutions of censure were withdrawn. The
victory was complete.

After the year 1838 John Quincy Adams had the
effective support of Joshua R. Giddings from the
Western Reserve, Ohio — who also fought a pitched
battle of his own which illustrates another phase
of the crusade against liberty. The ship *Creole* had
sailed from Baltimore to New Orleans in 1841 with
a cargo of slaves. The negroes mutinied on the
high seas, slew one man, gained possession of the
vessel, sailed to Nassau, and were there set free
by the British Government. Prolonged diplomatic

negotiations followed in which our Government held that, as slaves were property in the United States, they continued to be such on the high seas. In the midst of the controversy, Giddings introduced a resolution into the House, declaring that slavery, being an abridgment of liberty, could exist only under local rules, and that on the high seas there can be no slavery. For this act Giddings was arraigned and censured by the House. He at once resigned, but was reëlected with instructions to continue the fight for freedom of debate in the House.

In the campaign against the rights of freemen mob violence was first employed, but in the South the weapon of repressive legislation was soon substituted, and this was powerfully supplemented by social and religious ostracism. Except in a few districts in the border States, these measures were successful. Public profession of abolitionism was suppressed. The violence of the mob was of much longer duration in the North and reached its height in the years 1834 and 1835. But Northern mobs only quickened the zeal of the abolitionists and made converts to their cause. The attempt to substitute repressive state legislation had the same effect, and the use of church authority for making an end of the agitation for human liberty was only temporarily influential.

As early as 1838 the Presbyterian Church was divided over questions of doctrine into Old School and New School Presbyterians. This served to forestall the impending division on the slavery question. The Old School in the South became pro-slavery and the New School in the North became anti-slavery. At the same time the Methodist Church of the entire country was beset by a division on the main question. In 1844 Southern Methodist Episcopalian conferences resolved upon separation and committed themselves to the defense of slavery. The division in the Methodist Church was completed in 1846. A corresponding division took place in the Baptist Church in 1845. The controversy was dividing the country into a free North and an enslaved South, and Southern white men as well as negroes were threatened with subjection to the demands of the dominant institution.

CHAPTER VI

THE SLAVERY ISSUE IN POLITICS

SOME who opposed mob violence became active abolitionists; others were led to defend the rights of abolitionists because to do otherwise would encourage anarchy and general disorder. The same was true of those who defended the right of petition and the free use of the mails and the entire list of the fundamental rights of freemen which were threatened by the crusade against abolitionists. Birney's contention that unless the slave is freed no one can be free was thus vindicated: the issue involved vastly more than the mere emancipation of slaves.

The attack made in defense of slavery upon the rights of freemen was early recognized as involving civil war unless peaceable emancipation could be attained. So soon as John Quincy Adams faced the new spirit in Congress, he was convinced that it meant probable war. As early as May, 1836, he warned the South, saying: "From the instant that your slaveholding States become the theater of war, civil, servile, or foreign, from that moment the war powers of the Constitution extend to interference with the institution of slavery." This sentiment he reiterated and amplified on various occasions. The South was duly warned that an attempt to disrupt the Union would involve a war of which emancipation would be one of the consequences. With the exception of Garrison and a few of his personal followers, abolitionists were unionists: they stood for the perpetual union of the States.

This is not the place to give an extended account of the Mexican War.[1] There are, however, certain incidents connected with the annexation of Texas and the resulting war which profoundly affected the crusade against slavery. Both Lundy and Birney in their missions to promote emancipation through the process of colonization believed that they had unearthed a plan on the part of Southern leaders to acquire territory from Mexico for the purpose of extending slavery. This discovery coincided with the suppression of abolition propaganda in the South. Hitherto John Quincy Adams

[1] See *Texas and the Mexican War* (in *The Chronicles of America*).

had favored the western expansion of our territory. He had labored diligently to make the Rio Grande the western boundary of the Louisiana Purchase at the time of the treaty with Spain in 1819. But though in 1825 he had supported a measure to purchase Texas from Mexico, under the new conditions he threw himself heartily against the annexation of Texas, and in 1838 he defeated in the House of Representatives a resolution favoring annexation. To this end Adams occupied the morning hour of the House each day from the 16th of June to the 7th of July, within two days of the time fixed for adjournment. This was only a beginning of his fight against the extension of slavery. There was no relenting in his opposition to pro-slavery demands until he was stricken down with paralysis in the streets of Boston, in November, 1846. He never again addressed a public assembly. But he continued to occupy his seat in Congress until February 23, 1848.

The debate inaugurated in Congress by Adams and others over the extension of slave territory rapidly spread to the country at large, and interest in the question became general. Abolitionists were thereby greatly stimulated to put into practice their professed duty of seeking to accomplish

their ends by political action. Their first effort was
to secure recognition in the regular parties. The
Democrats answered in their platform of 1840 by
a plank specifically denouncing the abolitionists,
and the Whigs proved either noncommital or
unfriendly. The result was that abolitionists organized a party of their own in 1840 and nominated
James G. Birney for the Presidency. Both of the
older parties during this campaign evaded the issue
of the annexation of Texas. In 1844 the Whigs
again refrained from giving in their platform any
official utterance on the Texas issue, though they
were understood to be opposed to annexation.
The Democrats adroitly asserted in their platform
their approval of the *re*-annexation of Texas and *re*-
occupation of Oregon. There was a shadowy prior
claim to both these regions, and by combining
them in this way the party avoided any odious
partiality towards the acquisition of slave territory. But the voters in both parties had become
interested in the specific question whether the
country was to enter upon a war of conquest whose
primary object should be the extension of slavery.
In the North it became generally understood that
a vote for Henry Clay, the Whig candidate, was an
expression of opposition to annexation. This issue,

however, was not made clear in the South.   In the absence of telegraph and daily paper it was quite possible to maintain contradictory positions in different sections of the country.   But since the Democrats everywhere openly favored annexation, the election of their candidate, James K. Polk, was generally accepted as a popular approval of the annexation of Texas.   Indeed, action immediately followed the election and, before the President-elect had been inaugurated, the joint resolution for the annexation of Texas passed both Houses of Congress.

The popular vote was almost equally divided between Whigs and Democrats.   Had the vote for Birney, who was again the candidate of the Liberty party, been cast for Clay electors, Clay would have been chosen President.   The Birney vote was over sixty-two thousand.   The Liberty party, therefore, held the balance of power and determined the result of the election.

The Liberty party has often been censured for defeating the Whigs at this election of 1844.   But many incidents, too early forgotten by historians, go far to justify the course of the leaders.   Birney and Clay were at one time members of the same party.   They were personal friends, and as slaveholders they shared the view that slavery was a menace to the country and ought to be abolished. It was just fourteen years before this election that Birney made a visit to Clay to induce him to accept the leadership of an organized movement to abolish slavery in Kentucky. Three years later, when Birney returned to Kentucky to do himself what Henry Clay had refused to do, he became convinced that the reaction which had taken place in favor of slavery was largely due to Clay's influence. This was a common impression among active abolitionists. It is not strange, therefore, that they refused to support him as a candidate for the Presidency, and it is not at all certain that his election in 1844 would have prevented the war with Mexico.

Northern Whigs accused the Democrats of fomenting a war with Mexico with the intention of gaining territory for the purpose of extending slavery. Democrats denied that the annexation of Texas would lead to war, and many of them proclaimed their opposition to the farther extension of slavery. In harmony with this sentiment, when President Polk asked for a grant of two million dollars to aid in making a treaty with Mexico, they attached to the bill granting the amount a proviso

to the effect that slavery should forever be prohibited in any territory which might be obtained
from Mexico by the contemplated treaty.   The
proviso was written by an Ohio Democrat and was
introduced in the House by David A. Wilmot, a
Pennsylvania Democrat, after whom it is known.
It passed the House by a fair majority with the
support of both Whigs and Democrats.   At the
time of the original introduction in August, 1846,
the Senate did not vote upon the measure.   Davis
of Massachusetts moved its adoption but in-
advertently prolonged his speech in its favor until
the hour for adjournment.   Hence there was no
vote on the subject.   Subsequently the proviso
in a new form again passed the House but failed
of adoption in the Senate.

During the war the Wilmot Proviso was the
subject of frequent debate in Congress and of continuous debate throughout the country until the
treaty with Mexico was signed in 1848.   A vast
territory had been acquired as a result of the war,
and no decision had been reached as to whether it
should remain free or be opened to settlement by
slave-owners.   Another presidential election was
at hand.   For fully ten years there had been ever-
increasing excitement over the question of the

limitation or the extension of slavery. This had clearly become the topic of supreme interest throughout the country, and yet the two leading parties avoided the issue. Their own membership was divided. Northern Democrats, many of them, were decidedly opposed to slavery extension. Southern Whigs with equal intensity favored the extension of slavery into the new territory. The platforms of the two parties were silent on the subject. The Whigs nominated Taylor, a Southern general who had never voted their party ticket, but they made no formal declaration of principles. The Democrats repeated with colorless additions their platforms of 1840 and 1844 and sought to win the election with a Northern man, Lewis Cass of Michigan, as candidate.

There was, therefore, a clear field for a party having fully defined views to express on a topic of commanding interest. The cleavage in the Democratic party already begun by the debate over the Wilmot Proviso was farther promoted by a factional division of New York Democrats. Martin Van Buren became the leader of the liberal faction, the "Barnburners," who nominated him for President at a convention at Utica. The spirit of independence now seized disaffected Whigs and

Democrats everywhere in the North and Northwest. Men of anti-slavery proclivities held nonpartizan meetings and conventions. The movement finally culminated in the famous Buffalo convention which gave birth to the Free-soil party. The delegates of all political persuasions united on the one principle of opposition to slavery. They adopted a ringing platform closing with the words: "*Resolved*, That we inscribe on our banner 'Free Soil, Free Speech, Free Labor, and Free Men,' and under it will fight on, and fight ever, until a triumphant victory shall reward our exertions." They accepted Van Buren as their candidate. The vote at the ensuing election was more than fourfold that given to Birney in 1844. The Van Buren supporters held the balance of power between Whigs and Democrats in twelve States. Taylor was elected by the vote of New York, which except for the division in the party would have gone to Cass. There was no longer any doubt of the fact that a political force had arisen which could no longer be ignored by the ruling parties. One of the parties must either support the new issue or give place to a party which would do so.

A political party for the defense of liberty was the fulfillment of the aspirations of all earnest anti-slavery men and of all abolitionists not of the radical Garrisonian persuasion. The national anti-slavery societies were for the most part limited in their operations to the Atlantic seaboard. The West organized local and state associations with little reference to the national association. When the disruption occurred between Garrison and his opponents in 1840, the Western abolitionists continued their former methods of local organization. They recognized no divisions in their ranks and continued to work in harmony with all who in any way opposed the institution of slavery. The political party was their first really effective national organization. Through party committees, caucuses, and conventions, they became a part of the forces that controlled the nation. The older local clubs and associations were either displaced by the party or became mere adjuncts to the party.

The lines for political action were now clearly defined. In the States emancipation should be accomplished by state action. With a few individual exceptions the leaders conceded that Congress had no power to abolish slavery in the States. Upon the general Government they urged the duty of abolishing both slavery and the slave-trade in the District of Columbia and in all areas under

direct federal control. They further urged upon
the Government the strict enforcement of the laws
prohibiting the foreign slave-trade and the enactment of laws forbidding the interstate slave-trade.
The constitutionality of these main lines of action
has been generally conceded.

Abolitionists were pioneers in the formulation of
political platforms. The declaration of principles
drawn up by Garrison in 1833 and adopted by the
American Anti-Slavery Society was of the nature
of a political platform. The duty of voting in
furtherance of the policy of emancipation was in-
culcated. No platform was adopted for the first
political campaign, that of 1840; but four years
later there was an elaborate party platform of
twenty-one resolutions. Many things had happened in the eleven years intervening since the
declaration of principles of the American Anti-
Slavery Society. In the earlier platform the freedom of the slave appears as the primary object.
That of the Liberty party assumes the broad prin
ciple of human brotherhood as the foundation for a
democracy or a republic. It denies that the party
is organized merely to free the slave. Slaveholding
as the grossest form of despotism must indeed be
attacked first, but the aim of the party is to carry

the principle of equal rights into all social relations. It is not a sectional party nor a party organized for a single purpose. "It is not a new party, nor a third party, but it is the party of 1776, reviving the principles of that memorable era, and striving to carry them into practical application." The spirit of '76 rings, indeed, throughout the document, which declares that it was understood at the time of the Declaration and the Constitution that the existence of slavery was in derogation of the principles of American liberty. The implied faith of the Nation and the States was pledged to remove this stain upon the national character. Some States had nobly fulfilled that pledge; others shamelessly had neglected to do so.

These principles are reasserted in succeeding platforms. The later opponents of slavery in their principles and policies thus allied themselves with the founders of the republic. They claimed the right to continue to repeat the words of Washington and Jefferson and those of the members of the Virginia Legislature of 1832. No new doctrines were required. It was enough simply to reaffirm the fundamental principles of democracy.

The names attached to the party are significant. It was at first popularly styled the Abolition party, then officially in turn the Liberty party, the Free-soil party, and finally the Republican party. Republican was the name first applied to the Democratic party — the party of Jefferson. The term Democrat was gradually substituted under the leadership of Jackson before 1830. Some of the men who participated in the organization of the later Republican party had themselves been Republicans in the party of Jefferson. They not only accepted the name which Jefferson gave to his party, but they adopted the principles which Jefferson proclaimed on the subject of slavery, free soil, and human rights in general. This was the final stage in the identification of the later anti-slavery crusade with the earlier contest for liberty

7

CHAPTER VII

THE PASSING OF THE WHIG PARTY

THE middle of the last century was marked by many incidents which have left a permanent impress upon politics in general and upon the slavery question in particular. Europe was again in the throes of popular uprisings. New constitutions were adopted in France, Switzerland, Prussia, and Austria. Reactions in favor of autocracy in Austria and Germany sent multitudes of lovers of liberty to America. Kossuth, the Hungarian revolutionist, electrified American audiences by his appeals on behalf of the downtrodden in Europe. Already the world was growing smaller. America did not stop at the Pacific but crossed the ocean to establish permanent political and commercial relations with Japan and China.

The industries of the country were being reorganized to meet new conditions created by recent inventions. The electric telegraph was just coming into use, giving rise to a new era in communication. The discovery of gold in California in 1848 was followed by competing projects to construct railroads to the Pacific with Chicago and St. Louis as the rival eastern terminals. The telegraph, the railway, and the resulting industrial development proved great nationalizing influences. They served also to give increased emphasis to the contrast between the industries of the free and those of the slave States. The Census of 1850 became an effective anti-slavery argument.

The telegraph also gave new life to the public press. The presidential campaign of 1848 was the last one in which it was possible to carry on contradictory arguments in support of the same candidate. If slavery could not endure the test of untrammeled discussion when there were no means of rapid intercommunication such as the telegraph supplied, how could it contend against the revelations of the daily press with the new type of reporter and interviewer which was now developed?

It is a remarkable coincidence that in the midst of the passing of the old and the coming in of the new order there should be a change in the political leadership of the country. Webster, Clay, Calhoun, John Quincy Adams, not to mention others.

all died near the middle of the century, and their political power passed to younger men. Adams gave his blessing to a young friend and colaborer, William H. Seward of New York, intimating that he expected him to do much to curb the threatening power of the slaveholding oligarchy; while Andrew Jackson, who died earlier, had already conferred a like distinction upon young Stephen A. Douglas. There was no lack of aspirants for the fallen mantles.

John C. Calhoun continued almost to the day of his death to modify his interpretation of the Constitution in the interest of his section. As a young man he avowed protectionist principles. Becoming convinced that slave labor was not suited to manufacture, he urged South Carolina to declare the protective tariff laws null and void within her limits. When his section seemed endangered by the distribution of anti-slavery literature through the mail, he extemporized a theory that each State had a right to pass statutes to protect itself in such an emergency, in which case it became the duty of the general Government and of all other States to respect such laws. When it finally appeared that the territory acquired from Mexico was likely to remain free, the same statesman made further discoveries. He found that Congress had no right to exclude slavery from any Territory belonging to the United States; that the owners of slaves had equal rights with the owners of other property; that neither Congress nor a territorial authority had any power to exclude slaves from a Territory. This doctrine was accepted by extremists in the South and was finally embodied in the Dred Scott decision of 1857.

Abolitionists had meantime evolved a precisely contradictory theory. They asserted that the Constitution gave no warrant for property in man, except as held under state laws; that with this exception freedom was guaranteed to all; that Congress had no more right to make a slave than it had to make a king; and that it was the duty of Congress to maintain freedom in all the Territories. Extremists expressed the view that all past acts whereby slavery had been extended were unconstitutional and therefore void. Between these extreme conflicting views was every imaginable grade of opinion. The prevailing view of opponents of slavery, however, was in harmony with their past conduct and maintained that Congress had complete control over slavery in the Territories.

When the Mexican territory was acquired,

Stephen A. Douglas, as the experienced chairman of the Committee on Territories in the Senate, was already developing a theory respecting slavery in the Territories which was destined to play a leading part in the later crusade against slavery. Douglas was the most thorough-going of expansionists and would acknowledge no northern boundary on this side of the North Pole, no southern boundary nearer than Panama. He regarded the United States, with its great principle of local autonomy, as fitted to become eventually the United States of the whole world, while he held it to be an immediate duty to make it the United States of North America. As the son-in-law of a Southern planter in North Carolina, and as the father of sons who inherited slave property, Douglas, although born in Vermont, knew the South as did no other Northern statesman. He knew also the institution of slavery at first hand. As a pronounced expansionist and as the congressional leader in all matters pertaining to the Territories, he acquired detailed information as to the qualities of these new possessions, and he spoke, therefore, with a good degree of authority when he said, "If there was one inch of territory in the whole of our acquisitions from Mexico where slavery could exist, it was in the valleys of the Sacramento and the San Joaquin." But this region was at once pre-empted for freedom upon the discovery of gold.

Douglas did not admit that even the whole of Texas would remain dedicated to slavery. Some of the States to be formed from it would be free, by the same laws of climate and resources which determined that the entire West would remain free. Before the Mexican War the Senator had become convinced that the extension of slavery had reached its limit; that the Missouri Compromise was a dead letter except as a psychological palliative; that Nature had already ordained that slave labor should be forever excluded from all Western terri-tory both north and south of that line. His reply to Calhoun's contention that a balance must be maintained between slave and free States was that he had plans for forming seventeen new States out of the vast Western domains, every one of which would be free. And besides, said he, "we all look forward with confidence to the time when Dela-ware, Maryland, Virginia, Kentucky, and Missouri, and probably North Carolina and Tennessee will adopt a gradual system of emancipation." Doug-las was one of the first to favor the admission of California as a free State. According to the

Missouri Compromise law and the laws of Mexico, all Western territory was free, and he was opposed to interference with existing conditions. The Missouri Compromise was still held sacred. Finally, however, it was with Douglas's assistance that the Compromise measures of 1850 were passed, one of which provided for territorial Governments for Utah and New Mexico with the proviso that, when admitted as States, slavery should be permitted or prohibited as the citizens of those States should determine at the time. Congress refrained from any declaration as to slavery in the Territories. It was this policy of "non-intervention" which four years later furnished plausible excuse for the repeal of the Missouri Compromise.

It was not strange that there was general ignorance in all parts of the country as to the resources of the newly acquired territory. The rush to the goldfields precipitated action in respect to California. Before General Taylor, the newly elected President, was inaugurated, there was imminent need of an efficient government. An early act of the Administration was to send an agent to assist in the formation of a state Government, and a convention was immediately called to frame a constitution. By unanimous vote of the convention, slavery was excluded. The constitution was approved by popular vote and was presented to Congress for final acceptance in December, 1849.

In the meantime a great commotion had arisen among the people. Southern state legislatures passed resolutions demanding that the rights of their peculiar institution should be recognized in the new Territory. Northern legislatures responded with resolutions favoring the admission of California as a State and the application of the Wilmot Proviso to the remaining territory. Northern Democrats had very generally denied that the affair with Mexico had as a chief purpose the extension of slavery. Democrats therefore united with Whigs in maintaining the principle of free soil. In the South there was a corresponding fusion of the two parties in support of the sectional issue.

General concern prevailed as to the attitude of the Administration. Taylor's election had been effected by both a Southern and a Northern split in the Democratic party. Northern Democrats had voted for the Free-soil candidate because of the alleged pro-slavery tendencies of their own party. Southern Democrats voted for Taylor because of their distrust of Lewis Cass, their own candidate. Some

of these met in convention and formally nominated
Taylor, and Taylor accepted their nomination with
thanks.   Northern anti-slavery Whigs had a difficult task to keep their members in line.   There is
evidence that Taylor held the traditional Southern
view that the anti-slavery North was disposed to
encroach upon the rights of the South.   Meeting
fewer Northern Whig supporters, he became convinced that the more active spirit of encroachment
was in the pro-slavery South.   California needed a
state Government, and the President took the most
direct method to supply that need.   As the inhabitants were unanimous in their desire to exclude
slavery, their wish should be respected. New
Mexico was in a similar situation.   As slavery was
already excluded from the territory under Mexican
law, and as there was no wish on the part of the
inhabitants to introduce slavery, the President
recognized existing facts and made no change.
When Southern leaders projected a scheme to
enlarge the boundaries of Texas so as to extend
slavery over a large part of New Mexico, President
Taylor set a guard of United States troops to maintain the integrity of the Territory.   When a deputation of Southern Whigs endeavored to dissuade
him from his purpose, threatening a dissolution of

the Union and intimating that army officers would
refuse to act against citizens of Texas, the soldier
President replied that in such an event he would
take command in person and would hang any one
caught in acts of treason. When Henry Clay introduced an elaborate project for a compromise
between the North and the South, the President
insisted that each question should be settled on its
own merits and directed the forces of the Administration against any sort of compromise. The debate over Clay's Omnibus Bill was long and acrimonious. On July 4, 1850, the President seemed
triumphant. But upon that day, notwithstanding
his apparent robust health, he was stricken down
with an acute disease and died five days later.
With his passing, the opposing Whig faction came
into power. The so-called compromise measures
were at length one by one passed by Congress and
approved by President Fillmore.

California was admitted as a free State; but as a
palliative to the South, Congress passed bills for the
organization of territorial Governments for New
Mexico and Utah without positive declarations regarding the powers of the territorial Legislatures
over slavery. All questions relating to title to
slaves were to be left to the courts. Meantime it

was left in doubt whether Mexican law excluding slavery was still in force. Southern malcontents maintained that this act was a mere hoax, using words which suggested concession when no concession was intended. Northern anti-slavery men criticized the act as the entering wedge for another great surrender to the enemy. Because of the uncertainty regarding the meaning of the law and the false hopes likely to be created, they maintained that it was fitted to foment discord and prolong the period of distrust between the two sections. At all events such was its actual effect.

A third act in this unhappy series gave to Texas ten millions of dollars for the alleged surrender of claims to a part of New Mexico. This had little bearing on the general subject of compromise; yet anti-slavery men criticized it on the ground that the issue raised was insincere; that the appropriation was in fact a bribe to secure votes necessary to pass the other measures; that the bill was passed through Congress by shameless bribery, and that even the boundaries conceded to Texas involved the surrender of free territory.

The abolition of the slave-trade in the District of Columbia was supported by both sections of the country. The removal of the slave pens within

sight of the Capitol to a neighboring city deprived
the abolitionists of one of their weapons for effective agitation, but it did not otherwise affect the
position of slavery.

Of the five acts included in the compromise
measures, the one which provided for the return of
fugitive slaves was most effective in the promotion
of hostility between the two sections. During the
six months of debate on the Omnibus Bill, numerous bills were presented to take the place of the
law of 1793. Webster brought forward a bill which
provided for the use of a jury to establish the validity of a claim to an escaped slave. But that which
was finally adopted by a worn-out Congress is
characterized as one of the most barbarous pieces
of legislation ever enacted by a civilized country.
A single incident may indicate the nature of the
act. James Hamlet, for three years a resident of
New York City, a husband and a father and a
member of the Methodist Church, was seized eight
days after the law went into effect by order of the
agent of Mary Brown of Baltimore, cut off from
all communication with his friends, hurried before
a commissioner, and on *ex parte* testimony was delivered into the hands of the agent, by whom he
was handcuffed and secretly conveyed to Baltimore.

Mr. Rhodes accounts for the enactment in the following words: "If we look below the surface we shall find a strong impelling motive of the Southern clamor for this harsh enactment other than the natural desire to recover lost property. Early in the session it took air that a part of the game of the disunionists was to press a stringent fugitive slave law, for which no Northern man could vote; and when it was defeated, the North would be charged with refusal to carry out a stipulation of the Constitution. . . . The admission of California was a bitter pill for the Southern ultras, but they were forced to take it. The Fugitive Slave Law was a taunt and a reproach to that part of the North where the anti-slavery sentiment ruled supremely, and was deemed a partial compensation." Clay expressed surprise that States from which few slaves escaped demanded a more stringent law than Kentucky, from which many escaped.

Whatever may have been the motives leading to the enactment, its immediate effect was the elimination of one of the great national parties, thus paving the way for the formation of parties along sectional lines. Two years after the passage of the compromise acts the Democratic national convention assembled to nominate a candidate for the

Presidency. The platform adopted by the party promised a faithful execution of the acts known as the compromise measures and added "the act for reclaiming fugitives from service or labor included; which act, being designed to carry out an express provision of the Constitution, cannot, with fidelity thereto, be repealed nor so changed as to destroy or impair its efficiency." When this was read, the convention broke out in uproarious applause. Then there was a demand that it should be read again. Again there was loud applause. Why was there this demand that a law which every one knew had proved a complete failure should be made a permanent part of the Constitution? And why the ungovernable hilarity over the demand that its "efficiency" should never be impaired? Surely the motive was something other than a desire to recover lost property. Upon the Whig party had been fastened the odium for the enactment of the law, and the act unrepealed meant the death of the party. The Democrats saw good reason for laughter.

CHAPTER VIII

THE UNDERGROUND RAILROAD

WHEREVER there are slaves there are fugitives if there is an available place of refuge. The wilds of Florida were such a refuge during the early part of last century. When the Northern States became free, fugitive slaves began to escape thither, and Canada, when it could be reached, was, of course, the goal of perfect security and liberty for all.

A professed object of the early anti-slavery societies was to prevent the enslavement of free negroes and in other ways to protect their rights. During the process of emancipation in Northern States large numbers of colored persons were spirited off to the South and sold into slavery. At various places along the border there were those who made it their duty to guard the rights of negroes and to prevent kidnapping. These guardians of the border furnished a nucleus for the development of what was later known as the Underground Railroad.

In 1796 President Washington wrote a letter to a friend in New Hampshire with reference to obtaining the return of a negro servant. He was careful to state that the servant should remain unmolested rather than "excite a mob or riot or even uneasy sensations in the minds of well disposed citizens." The result was that the servant remained free. President Washington here assumed that "well disposed citizens" would oppose her return to slavery. Three years earlier the President had himself signed a bill to facilitate by legal process the return of fugitives escaping into other States. He was certainly aware that such an act was on the statute books when he wrote his request to his friend in New Hampshire, yet he expected that, if an attempt were made to remove the refugee by force, riot and resistance by a mob would be the result.

Not until after the foreign slave-trade had been prohibited and the domestic trade had been developed, and not until there was a pro-slavery reaction in the South which banished from the slave States all anti-slavery propaganda, did the systematic assistance rendered to fugitive slaves assume

8

any large proportions or arouse bitter resentment. It began in the late twenties and early thirties of the nineteenth century, extended with the spread of anti-slavery organization, and was greatly encouraged and stimulated by the enactment of the law of 1850.

The Underground Railroad was never coextensive with the abolition movement. There were always abolitionists who disapproved the practice of assisting fugitives, and others who took no part in it. Of those who were active participants, the larger proportion confined their activities to assisting those who had escaped and would take no part in seeking to induce slaves to leave their masters. Efforts of that kind were limited to a few individuals only.

Incidents drawn from the reminiscences of Levi Coffin, the reputed president of the Underground Railroad, may serve to illustrate the origin and growth of the system. He was seven years old when he first saw near his home in North Carolina a coffle of slaves being driven to the Southern market by a man on horseback with a long whip. "The driver was some distance behind with the wagon. My father addressed the slaves pleasantly and then asked, 'Well, boys, why do they chain you?' One of the men whose countenance betrayed unusual intelligence and whose expression denoted the deepest sadness replied: 'They have taken us from our wives and children and they chain us lest we should make our escape and go back to them.'" When Coffin was fifteen, he rendered assistance to a man in bondage. Having an opportunity to talk with the members of a gang in the hands of a trader bound for the Southern market, he learned that one of the company, named Stephen, was a freeman who had been kidnapped and sold. Letters were written to Northern friends of Stephen who confirmed his assertion. Money was raised in the Quaker meeting and men were sent to recover the negro. Stephen was found in Georgia and after six months was liberated.

During the year 1821 other incidents occurred in the Quaker community at New Garden, near Greensboro, North Carolina, which illustrate different phases of the subject. Jack Barnes was the slave of a bachelor who became so greatly attached to his servant that he bequeathed to him not only his freedom but also a large share of his property. Relatives instituted measures to break the will, and Jack in alarm took refuge among the Quakers at New Garden. The suit went against

the negro, and the newspapers contained adver-
tisements offering a hundred dollars for information which should result in his recovery. To
prevent his return to bondage, it was decided that
Jack should join a family of Coffins who were
moving to Indiana.

At the same time a negro by the name of Sam
had for several months been abiding in the Quaker
neighborhood. He belonged to a Mr. Osborne, a
prototype of Simon Legree, who was so notoriously
cruel that other slave-owners assisted in protecting
his victims. After the Coffins, with Jack, had been
on the road for a few days, Osborne learned that a
negro was with them and, feeling sure that it was
his Sam, he started in hot haste after them. This
becoming known to the Friends, young Levi Coffin
was sent after Osborne to forestall disaster. The
descriptions given of Jack and Sam were practically
identical and it was surmised that when Osborne
should overtake the party and discover his mistake,
he would seize Jack for the sake of the offered
reward. Coffin soon came up with Osborne and
decided to ride with him for a time to learn his
plans. In the course of their conversation, it was
finally agreed that Coffin should assist in the recovery of Sam. Osborne was also generous and

insisted that if it proved to be the other "nigger"
who was with the company, Coffin should have
half the reward.   How the young Quaker out-
witted the tyrant, gained his point, sent Jack on
his way to liberty, and at the same time retained
the confidence of Osborne so that upon their return
home he was definitely engaged to assist Osborne
in finding Sam, is a fascinating story.   The abolitionist won from the slaveholder the doubtful
compliment that "there was not a man in that
neighborhood worth a d——n to help him hunt his
negro except young Levi Coffin."

Sam was perfectly safe so long as Levi Coffin
was guide for the hunting-party, but matters were
becoming desperate.   For the fugitive something
had to be done.   Another family was planning to
move to Indiana, and in their wagon Sam was to be
concealed and thus conveyed to a free State.   The
business had now become serious.   The laws of the
State affixed the death penalty for stealing a slave.
At night when young Coffin and his father, with
Sam, were on their way to complete arrangements
for the departure, horsemen appeared in the road
near by.   They had only time to throw themselves
flat on the ground behind a log.   From the conversation overheard, they were assured that they

had narrowly escaped the night-riders on the lookout for stray negroes. The next year, 1822, Coffin himself joined a party going to Indiana by the southern route through Tennessee and Kentucky. In the latter State they were at one time overtaken by men who professed to be looking for a pet dog, but whose real purpose was to recover runaway slaves. They insisted upon examining the contents of the wagons, for in this way only a short time previous a fugitive had been captured.

These incidents show the origin of the system. The first case of assistance rendered a negro was not in itself illegal, but was intended merely to prevent the crime of kidnapping. The second was illegal in form, but the aid was given to one who, having been set free by will, was being reënslaved, it was believed, by an unjust decision of a court. The third was a case of outrageous abuse on the part of the owner. The negro Sam had himself gone to a trader begging that he would buy him and preferring to take his chances on a Mississippi plantation rather than return to his master. The trader offered the customary price and was met with the reply that he could have the rascal if he would wait until after the enraged owner had taken his revenge, otherwise the price would be twice the amount offered.   A large proportion of the fugitives belonged to this maltreated class. Others were goaded to escape by the prospect of deportation to the Gulf States.   The fugitives generally followed the beaten line of travel to the North and West.

In 1826 Levi Coffin became a merchant in Newport, Indiana, a town near the Ohio line not far from Richmond.   In the town and in its neighborhood lived a large number of free negroes who were the descendants of former slaves whom North Carolina Quakers had set free and had colonized in the new country.   Coffin found that these blacks were accustomed to assist fugitives on their way to Canada.   When he also learnt that some had been captured and returned to bondage merely through lack of skill on the part of the negroes, he assumed active operations as a conductor on the Underground Railroad.

Coffin used the Underground Railroad as a means of making converts to the cause.   One who berated him for negro-stealing was adroitly induced to meet a newly arrived passenger and listen to his pathetic story.   At the psychological moment the objector was skillfully led to hand the fugitive a dollar to assist him in reaching a place of safety.

Coffin then explained to this benevolent non-abolitionist the nature of his act, assuring him that he was liable to heavy damages therefor. The reply was in this case more forcible than elegant: "Damn it! You've got me!" This conversion he publicly proclaimed for the sake of its influence upon others. Many were the instances in which those of supposed pro-slavery convictions were brought face to face with an actual case of the threatened reënslavement of a human being escaping from bondage and were, to their own surprise overcome by the natural, humane sentiment which asserted itself. For example, a Cincinnati merchant, who at the time was supposed to be assisting one of his Southern customers to recover an escaped fugitive, was confronted at his own home by the poor half-starved victim. Yielding to the impulse of compassion, he gave the slave food and personal assistance and directed the destitute creature to a place of refuge.

The division in the Quaker meeting in Indiana with which Levi Coffin was intimately associated may serve to exemplify a corresponding attitude in other churches on the question of slavery. The Quakers availed themselves of the first great anti-slavery movement to rid themselves completely the burden. Their Society itself became an anti-slavery organization. Yet even so the Friends had differences of opinion as to fit methods of action. Not only did many of them disapprove of rendering aid to fugitives but they also objected to the use of the meeting-houses for anti-slavery lectures. The formation of the Liberty party served to accentuate the division. The great body of the Friends were anti-slavery Whigs.

A crisis in the affairs of the Society of Friends in the State of Indiana was reached in 1843 when the radicals seceded and organized an independent "Anti-Slavery Friends Society." Immediately there appeared in numerous localities duplicate Friends' meeting-houses. In and around one of these, distinguished as "Liberty Hall," were gathered those whose supreme religious interest was directed against the sin of slavery. Never was there a church division which involved less bad blood or sense of injury or injustice. Members of the same family attended separate churches without the least difference in their cordial relations. No important principle was involved; there were apparently good reasons for both lines of policy, and each party understood and respected the other's position. After the adoption of the

Fugitive Slave Law of 1850 and the passing of the Whig party, these differences disappeared, the separate organization was disbanded, and all Friends' meeting-houses became "liberty halls."

The disposition to aid the fugitive was by no means confined to the North nor to Quakers in the South. Richard Dillingham, a young Quaker who had yielded to the solicitations of escaped fugitives in Cincinnati and had undertaken a mission to Nashville, Tennessee, to rescue their relatives from a "hard master," was arrested with three stolen slaves on his hands. He made confession in open court and frankly explained his motives. The *Nashville Daily Gazette* of April 13, 1849, has words of commendation for the prisoner and his family and states that "he was not without the sympathy of those who attended the trial." Though Dillingham committed a crime to which the death penalty was attached in some of the States, the jury affixed the minimum penalty of three years' imprisonment for the offense. As Nashville was far removed from Quaker influence or any sort of anti-slavery propaganda, Dillingham was himself astonished and was profoundly grateful for the leniency shown him by Court, jury, and prosecutors. This incident occurred in the year before the adoption of the

Fugitive Slave Law of 1850. It is well known that in all times and places which were free from partizan bitterness there was a general natural sympathy for those who imperiled their life and liberty to free the slave. Throughout the South men of both races were ready to give aid to slaves seeking to escape from dangers or burdens which they regarded as intolerable. While such a man as Frederick Douglass, when still a slave, was an agent of the Underground Railroad, Southern anti-slavery people themselves were to a large extent the original projectors of the movement. Even members of the families of slaveholders have been known to assist fugitives in their escape to the North.

The fugitives traveled in various ways which were determined partly by geographical conditions and partly by the character of the inhabitants of a region. On the Atlantic coast, from Florida to Delaware, slaves were concealed in ships and were thus conveyed to free States. Thence some made their way towards Canada by steamboat or rail-road, though most made the journey on foot or, less frequently, in private conveyances. Stalwart slaves sometimes walked from the Gulf States to the free States, traveling chiefly by night and guided by the North Star. Having reached a free State, they found friends among those of their own race, or were taken in hand by officers of the Underground Railroad and were thus helped across the Canadian border.

From the seacoast the valley of the Connecticut River furnished a convenient route for completing the journey northward, though the way of the fugitives was often deflected to the Lake Champlain region. In later years, when New England became generally sympathetic, numerous lines of escape traversed that entire section. Other courses extended northward from the vicinity of Philadelphia, Delaware, and Maryland. Here, through the center of American Quakerdom, all conditions favored the escape of fugitives, for slavery and freedom were at close quarters. The activities of the Quakers, who were at first engaged merely in preventing the reënslavement of those who had a legal right to freedom, naturally expanded until aid was given without reservation to any fugitive. From Philadelphia as a distributing point the route went by way of New York and the Hudson River or up the river valleys of eastern Pennsylvania through western New York.

In addition to the routes to freedom which the

seacoast and river valleys afforded, the Appalachian chain of mountains formed an attractive high-
way of escape from slavery, though these mountain
paths lead us to another branch of our subject
not immediately connected with the Underground
Railroad — the escape from bondage by the initiative of the slaves themselves or by the aid of their
own people. Mountains have always been a refuge
and a defense for the outlaw, and the few dwellers
in this almost unknown wilderness were not in-
frequently either indifferent or friendly to the
fugitives. The escaped slaves might, if they chose,
adopt for an indefinite time the free life of the hills;
but in most cases they naturally drifted northward
for greater security until they found themselves
in a free State. Through the mountainous regions
of Virginia many thus escaped, and they were induced to remain there by the example and advice
of residents of their own color. The negroes themselves excelled all others in furnishing places of
refuge to fugitives from slavery and in concealing
their status. For this reason John Brown and his
associates were influenced to select this region for
their great venture in 1859.

But there were other than geographical conditions which helped to determine the direction

of the lines of the Underground Railroad. West of the Alleghanies are the broad plains of the Mississippi Valley, and in this great region human elements rather than physical characteristics proved influential. Northern Ohio was occupied by settlers from the East, many of whom were anti-slavery. Southern Ohio was populated largely by Quakers and other people from the slave States who abhorred slavery. On the east and south the State bordered on slave territory, and every part of the region was traversed by lines of travel for the slave. In eastern and northern Indiana a favorable attitude prevailed. Southwestern Indiana, however, and southern Illinois were occupied by those less friendly to the slave, so that in these sections there is little evidence of systematic aid to fugitives. But with St. Louis, Missouri, as a starting-point, northern Illinois became honeycombed with refuges for patrons of the Underground Railroad. The negro also found friends in all the settled portions of Iowa, and at the outbreak of the Civil War a lively traffic was being developed, extending from Lawrence, Kansas, to Keokuk, Iowa.

There is respectable authority for a variety of opinions as to the requirements of the rendition clause in the Constitution and of the Act of Congress of 1793 to facilitate the return of fugitives from service or labor; but there is no respectable authority in support of the view that neither the spirit nor the letter of the law was violated by the supporters of the Underground Railroad. This was a source of real weakness to anti-slavery leaders in politics. It was always true that only a small minority of their numbers were actual violators of the law, yet such was their relation to the organized anti-slavery movement that responsibility attached to all. The platform of the Liberty party for 1844 declared that the provisions of the Constitution for reclaiming fugitive slaves were dangerous to liberty and ought to be abrogated. It further declared that the members of the party would treat these provisions as void, because they involved an order to commit an immoral act. The platform thus explicitly committed the party to the support of the policy of rendering aid to fugitive slaves. Four years later the platform of the Free-soil party contained no reference whatever to fugitive slaves, but that of 1852 denounced the Fugitive Slave Act of 1850 as repugnant to the Constitution and the spirit of Christianity and denied its binding force on the American people.

The Republican platform of 1856 made no reference to the subject.

The Underground Railroad filled an insignificant place in the general plan for emancipation,
even in the minds of the directors. It was a lesser
task preparatory to the great work. As to the
numbers of slaves who gained their freedom by
means of it, there is a wide range of opinion. Statements in Congress by Southern members that a
hundred thousand had escaped must be regarded
as gross exaggerations. In any event the loss was
confined chiefly to the border States. Besides, it
has been stated with some show of reason that
the danger of servile insurrection was diminished
by the escape of potential leaders.

From the standpoint of the great body of anti-
slavery men who expected to settle the slavery
question by peaceable means, it was a calamity of
the first magnitude that, just at the time when
conditions were most favorable for transferring the
active crusade from the general Government to the
separate States, public attention should be directed
to the one point at which the conflict was most
acute and irrepressible.

Previous to 1850 there had been no general
acrimonious debate in Congress on the rendition of

fugitive slaves. About half of those who had previously escaped from bondage had not taken the trouble to go as far as Canada, but were living at peace in the Northern States. Few people at the North knew or cared anything about the details of a law that had been on the statute books since 1793. Members of Congress were duly warned of the dangers involved in any attempt to enforce a more stringent law than the previous act which had proved a dead letter. To those who understood the conditions, the new law also was doomed to failure. So said Senator Butler of South Carolina. An attempt to enforce it would be met by violence.

This prediction came true. The twenty thousand potential victims residing in Northern States were thrown into panic. Some rushed off to Canada; others organized means for protection. A father and son from Baltimore came to a town in Pennsylvania to recover a fugitive. An alarm was sounded; men, mostly colored, rushed to the protection of the one whose liberty was threatened. Two Quakers appeared on the scene and warned the slave-hunters to desist and upon their refusal one slave-hunter was instantly killed and the other wounded. The fugitive was conveyed to a place of safety, and to the murderers no punishment was meted out, though the general Government made strenuous efforts to discover and punish them. In New York, though Gerrit Smith and a local clergyman with a few assistants rescued a fugitive from the officers of the law and sent him to Canada, openly proclaiming and justifying the act, no attempt was made to punish the offenders.

After a dozen years of intense and ever-increasing excitement, when other causes of friction between North and South had apparently been removed and good citizens in the two sections were rejoicing at the prospect of an era of peace and harmony, public attention was concentrated upon the one problem of conduct which would not admit of peaceable legal adjustment. Abolitionists had always been stigmatized as lawbreakers whose aim was the destruction of slavery in utter disregard of the rights of the States. This charge was absolutely false; their settled program involved full recognition of state and municipal control over slavery. Yet after public attention had become fixed upon conduct on the part of the abolitionists which was illegal, it was difficult to escape the implication that their whole course was illegal. This was the tragic significance of the Fugitive Slave Act of 1850.

CHAPTER IX

BOOKS AS ANTI-SLAVERY WEAPONS

WHITTIER offered up "thanks for the fugitive slave law; for it gave occasion for *Uncle Tom's Cabin*." Mrs. Harriet Beecher Stowe had been mistress of a station on the Underground Railroad at Cincinnati, the storm-center of the West, and out of her experience she has transmitted to the world a knowledge of the elemental and tragic human experiences of the slaves which would otherwise have been restricted to a select few. The mistress of a similar station in eastern Indiana, though she held novel reading a deadly sin, said: "*Uncle Tom's Cabin* is not a novel, it is a record of facts. I myself have listened to the same stories" The reading public in all lands soon became sympathetic participants in the labors of those who, in defiance of law, were lending a hand to the aspirants for liberty. At the time of the publication of the story in book form in March, 1852, America was being profoundly stirred by the stories of fugitives who had escaped from European despotism. Mrs. Stowe refers to these incidents in her question: "When despairing Hungarian fugitives make their way, against all the search-warrants and authorities of their lawful governments to America, press and political cabinet ring with applause and welcome. When despairing African fugitives do the same thing — it is — what *is* it?" Little did she think that when the eloquence of the Hungarian refugee had been forgotten, the story of Eliza and Uncle Tom would ring throughout the world.

The book did far more than vindicate the conduct of those who rendered assistance to the fugitive from slavery; it let in daylight upon the essential nature of slavery. Humane and just masters are shown to be forced into participation in acts which result in intolerable cruelty. Full justice is done to the noble and admirable character of Southern slave-owners. The author had been a guest in the home of the "Shelbys," in Kentucky. She had taken great pains to understand the Southern point of view on the subject of slavery; she had entered into the real trials and difficulties involved in any plan of emancipation. St. Clair, speaking to Miss Ophelia, his New England cousin, says:

If we emancipate, are you willing to educate? How many families of your town would take in a negro man or woman, teach them, bear with them, and seek to make them Christians? How many merchants would take Adolph, if I wanted to make him a clerk; or mechanics, if I wanted to teach him a trade? If I wanted to put Jane and Rosa to a school, how many schools are there in the Northern States that would take them in? How many families that would board them? and yet they are as white as many a woman north or south. You see, cousin, I want justice done us. We are in a bad position. We are the more *obvious* oppressors of the negro; but the unchristian prejudice of the north is an oppressor almost equally severe.

Throughout the book the idea is elaborated in many ways. Miss Ophelia is introduced for the purpose of contrasting Northern ignorance and New England prejudice with the patience and forbearance of the better class of slave-owners of the South. The genuine affection of an unspoiled child for negro friends is made especially emphatic. Miss Ophelia objected to Eva's expressions of devotion to Uncle Tom. Her father insists that his daughter shall not be robbed of the free utterance of her high regard, observing that "the child is the only true democrat." There is only one Simon Legree in the book, and he is of New England extraction. The story is as distinctly intended to inform Northern ignorance and to remove Northern prejudice as it is to justify the conduct of abolitionists.

What was the effect of the publication? In European countries far removed from local, partizan prejudice, it was immediately received as a great revelation of the spirit of liberty. It was translated into twenty-three different languages. So devoted were the Italians to the reading of the story that there was earnest effort to suppress its circulation. As a drama it proved a great success, not only in America and England but in France and other countries as well. More than a million copies of the story were sold in the British Empire. Lord Palmerston avers that he had not read a novel for thirty years, yet he read *Uncle Tom's Cabin* three times and commended the book for the statesmanship displayed in it.

What is in the story to call forth such commendation from the cold-blooded English statesman? The book revealed, in a way fitted to carry conviction to every unprejudiced reader, the impossibility of uniting slavery with freedom under the same Government. Either all must be free or the mass subject to the few — or there is actual war. This principle is finely brought out in the predica-

ment of the Quaker confronted by a fugitive with
wife and child who had seen a sister sold and conveyed to a life of shame on a Southern plantation.
"Am I going to stand by and see them take my wife
and sell her?" exclaimed the negro. "No, God
help me! I'll fight to the last breath before they
shall take my wife and son. Can you blame me?"
To which the Quaker replied: "Mortal man cannot blame thee, George. Flesh and blood could not
do otherwise. 'Woe unto the world because of of-
fences but woe unto them through whom the of-
fence cometh.'" "Would not even you, sir, do the
same, in my place?" "I pray that I be not tried."
And in the ensuing events the Quaker played an
important part.

Laws enacted for the protection of slave property are shown to be destructive of the fundamental rights of freemen; they are inhuman. The Ohio
Senator, who in his lofty preserve at the capital of
his country could discourse eloquently of his readi-
ness to keep faith with the South in the matter of
the faithful execution of the Fugitive Slave Law,
becomes, when at home with his family, a flagrant
violator of the law. Elemental human nature is
pitted against the apparent interests of a few individual slave-owners.

The story of Uncle Tom placed all supporters of the new law on the defensive. It was read by all classes North and South. *Uncle Tom's Cabin as it is* was called forth from the South as a reply to Mrs. Stowe's book, and there ensued a general discussion of the subject which was on the whole enlightening. Yet the immediate political effect of the publication was less than might have been expected from a book so widely read and discussed. Its appearance early in the decade did not prevent the apparent pro-slavery reaction already described. But Mr. Rhodes calls attention to the different impression which the book made upon adults and boys. Hardened sinners in partizan politics could read the book, laugh and weep over the passing incidents, and then go on as if nothing had happened. Not so with the thirteen-year-old boy. He never could be the same again. The Republican party of 1860 was especially successful in gaining the first vote of the youthful citizen and undoubtedly owed much of its influence to *Uncle Tom's Cabin.*

Two lines of attack were rapidly rendering impossible the continuance of slavery in the United States. Mrs. Stowe gave effective expression to the moral, religious, and humanitarian sentiment against slavery. In the year in which her work was published, Frederick Law Olmsted began his extended journeys throughout the South. He represents the impartial scientific observer. His books were published during the years 1856, 1857, and 1861. They constitute in their own way an indictment against slavery quite as forcible as that of *Uncle Tom's Cabin*, but an indictment that rests chiefly upon the blighting influence of the institution of slavery upon agriculture, manufactures, and the general industrial and social order. The crisis came too soon for these publications to have any marked effect upon the issue. Their appeal was to the deliberate and thoughtful reader, and political control had already drifted into the hands of those who were not deliberate and composed.

In 1857, however, there appeared a book which did exert a marked influence upon immediate political issues. There is no evidence that Hinton Rowan Helper, the author of *The Impending Crisis*, had any knowledge of the writings of Olmsted; but he was familiar with Northern anti-slavery literature. "I have considered my subject more particularly," he states in his preface, "with reference to its economic aspects as regards the whites — not with reference, except in a very slight degree, to its humanitarian or religious aspects. To the latter side of the question, Northern writers have already done full and timely justice. . . . Yankee wives have written the most popular anti-slavery litera-ture of the day. Against this I have nothing to say; it is all well enough for women to give the fictions of slavery; men should give the facts." He denies that it had been his purpose to cast unmerited opprobium upon slaveholders; yet a sense of per-sonal injury breathes throughout the pages. If he had no intention of casting unmerited opprobrium upon slaveholders, it is difficult to imagine what language he could have used if he had undertaken to pass the limit of deserved reprobation. In this regard the book is quite in line with the style of Southern utterance against abolitionists.

Helper belonged to a slaveholding family, for a hundred years resident in the Carolinas. The dedication is significant. It is to three personal friends from three slave States who at the time were residing in California, in Oregon, and in Wash-ington Territory, "and to the non-slaveholding whites of the South generally, whether at home or abroad." Out of the South had come the inspira-tion for the religious and humanitarian attack upon slavery. From the same source came the call for relief of the poverty-stricken white victims of the institution.

Helper's book revived the controversy which had been forcibly terminated a quarter of a century before. He resumes the argument of the members of the Virginia legislature of 1832. He reprints extended selections from that memorable debate and then, by extended references to later official reports, points out how slavery is impoverishing the South. The South is shown to have continuously declined, while the North has made immense gains. In a few years the relation of the South to the North would resemble that of Poland to Russia or of Ireland to England. The author sees no call for any arguments against slavery as an economic system; he would simply bring the earlier characterization of the situation down to date.

Helper differs radically from all earlier speakers and writers in that he outlines a program for definite action. He estimates that for the entire South there are seven white non-slaveholders for every three slaveholders. He would organize these non-slaveholding whites into an independent political party and would hold a general convention of non-slaveholders from every slave State to adopt measures to restrain "the diabolical excesses of the oligarchy" and to annihilate slavery. Slave-holders should be entirely excluded from any share in government. They should be treated as criminals ostracized from respectable society. He is careful to state, however, that by slaveholder he does not mean such men as Benton of Missouri and many others throughout the slave States who retain the sentiments on the slavery question of the "immortal Fathers of the Republic." He has in mind only the new order of owners, who have determined by criminal methods to inflict the crime of slavery upon an overwhelming majority of their white fellow-citizens.

The publication of *The Impending Crisis* created a profound sensation among Southern leaders. So long as the attack upon the peculiar institution emanated from the North, the defenders had the full benefit of local prejudice and resentment against outside intrusion. Helper was himself a thorough-going believer in state rights. Slavery was to be abolished, as he thought, by the action of the separate States. Here he was in accord with Northern abolitionists. If such literature as Helper's volume should find its way into the South, it would be no longer possible to palm off upon the unthinking public the patent falsehood that abolitionists of the North were attempting to impose by force a change in Southern institutions. All that Southern abolitionists ever asked was the privilege of remaining at home in their own South in the full exercise of their constitutional rights.

Southern leaders were undoubtedly aware of the concurrent publications of travelers and newspaper reporters, of which Olmsted's books were conspicuous examples. Olmsted and Helper were both sources of proof that slavery was bringing the South to financial ruin. The facts were getting hold of the minds of the Southern people. The debate which had been adjourned was on the eve of being resumed. Complete suppression of the new scientific industrial argument against slavery seemed to slave-owners to furnish their only defense

The Appalachian ranges of mountains drove a wedge of liberty and freedom from Pennsylvania almost to the Gulf. In the upland regions slavery could not flourish. There was always enmity between the planters of the coast and the dwellers on the upland. The slaveholding oligarchy had always ruled, but the day of the uplanders was at hand. This is the explanation of the veritable panic which Helper's publication created. A debate which should follow the line of this old division between the peoples of the Atlantic slave States would, under existing conditions, be fatal to the institution of slavery. West Virginia did become a free State at the first opportunity. Counties in western North Carolina claim to have furnished a larger proportion of their men to the Union army than any other counties in the country. Had the plan for peaceable emancipation projected by abolitionists been permitted to take its course, the uplands of South Carolina would have been pitted against the lowlands, and Senator Tillman would have appeared as a rampant abolitionist. There might have been violence, but it would have been confined to limited areas in the separate States. Had the crisis been postponed, there surely would have been a revival of abolitionism within the Southern States. Slavery in Missouri was already approaching a crisis. Southern leaders had long foreseen that the State would abolish slavery if a free State should be established on the western boundary. This was actually taking place. Kansas was filling up with free-state settlers and, by the act of its own citizens, a few years later did abolish slavery.

Republicans naturally made use of Helper's book for party purposes. A cheap abridged edition was brought out. Several Republican leaders were induced to sign their names to a paper commending the publication. Among these was John Sherman of Ohio, who in the organization of the newly elected House of Representatives in 1859 was the leading candidate of the Republicans for the speakership. During the contest the fact that his name was on this paper was made public, and Southern leaders were furious. Extracts were read to prove that the book was incendiary. Millson of Virginia said that "one who consciously, deliberately, and of purpose lends his name and influence to the propagation of such writings is not only not fit to be speaker, but he is not fit to live." It is one of the ironies of the situation that the passage selected to prove the incendiary character of the book is almost a literal quotation from the debate in the Virginia Legislature of 1832.

CHAPTER X

"BLEEDING KANSAS"

BOTH the leading political parties were, in the campaign of 1852, fully committed to the acceptance of the so-called Compromise of 1850 as a final settlement of the slavery question; both were committed to the support of the Fugitive Slave Act. The Free-soil party, with John P. Hale as its candidate, did make a vigorous attack upon the Fugitive Slave Act, and opposed all compromises respecting slavery, but Free-soilers had been to a large extent reabsorbed into the Democratic party, their vote of 1852 being only about half that of 1848. Though the Whig vote was large and only about two hundred thousand less than that of the Democrats, yet it was so distributed that the Whigs carried only four States, Massachusetts, Vermont, Kentucky, and Tennessee. The other States gave a Democratic plurality.

Had there been time for readjustment, the Whig

party might have recovered lost ground, but no time was permitted. There was in progress in Missouri a political conflict which was already commanding national attention. Thomas H. Benton, for thirty years a Senator from Missouri, and a national figure, was the storm-center. His enemies accused him of being a Free-soiler, an abolitionist in disguise. He was professedly a stanch and uncompromising unionist, a personal and political opponent of John C. Calhoun. According to his own statement he had been opposed to the extension of slavery since 1804, although he had advocated the admission of Missouri with a pro-slavery constitution in 1820. He was, from the first, senior Senator from the State, and by a peculiar combination of influences incurred his first defeat for reëlection in 1851.

Benton's defeat in the Missouri Legislature was largely the result of national pro-slavery influences. In a former chapter, reference was made to the Ohio River as furnishing a "providential argument against slavery." The Mississippi River as the eastern boundary of Missouri furnished a like argument, but on the north not even a prairie brook separated free labor in Iowa from slave labor in Missouri. The inhabitants of western Missouri, realizing that the tenure of their peculiar institution was becoming weaker in the east and north, early became convinced that the organization of a free State along their western boundary would be followed by the abolition of slavery in their own State.   This condition attracted the attention of the national guardians of pro-slavery interests. Calhoun, Davis, Breckinridge, Toombs, and others were in constant communication with local leaders. A certain Judge W. C. Price, a religious fanatic, and a pro-slavery devotee, was induced to visit every part of the State in 1844, calling the attention of all slaveholders to the perils of the situation and preparing the way for the repeal of the Missouri Compromise.   Senator Benton, who was approached on the subject, replied in such a way that all radical defenders of slavery, both national leaders and local politicians, were moved to unite for his political defeat.

David R. Atchison, junior Senator from Missouri, had been made the leader of the pro-slavery forces.   The defeat of Benton in the Missouri Legislature did not end the strife.   He at once became a candidate for Atchison's place in the election which was to occur in 1855, and he was in the meantime elected to the House of Representatives in

1852. The most telling consideration in Benton's favor was the general demand, in which he himself joined, for the immediate organization of the western territory in order to facilitate the building of a system of railways reaching the Pacific, with St. Louis as the point of departure. For a time, in 1852 and 1853, Benton was apparently triumphant, and Atchison was himself willing to consent to the organization of the new territory with slavery excluded. The national leaders, however, were not of the same mind. The real issue was the continuance of slavery in the State; the one thing which must not be permitted was the transfer of anti-slavery agitation to the separate States. Henry Clay's proposal of 1849 to provide for gradual emancipation in Kentucky was bitterly resented. It had long been an axiom with the slavocracy that the institution would perish unless it had the opportunity to expand. Out of this conviction arose Calhoun's famous theory that slave-owners had under the Constitution an equal right with the owners of all other forms of property in all the Territories. The theory itself assumed that the act prohibiting slavery in the territory north of the southern boundary of Missouri was unconstitutional and void.

But this theory had not yet received judicial sanction, and the time was at hand when the question of freedom or slavery in the western territory was to be determined. Between March and December, 1853, the discovery was made that the Act of 1850 organizing the Territories of New Mexico and Utah had superseded the Compromise of 1820; that a principle had been recognized applicable to all the Territories; that all were open to settlement on equal terms to slaveholders and non-slaveholders; that the subject of slavery should be removed from Congress to the people of the Territories; and that they should decide, either when a territorial legislature was organized or at the time of the adoption of a constitution preparatory to statehood, whether or not slavery should be authorized. These ideas found expression in various newspapers during the month of December, 1853. Though the authorship of the new theory is still a matter of dispute, it is well known that Stephen A. Douglas became its chief sponsor and champion. The real motives and intentions of Douglas himself and of many of his supporters will always remain obscure and uncertain. But no uncertainty attaches to the motives of Senator Atchison and the leaders of the Calhoun section of the

Democratic party. For ten years at least they had
been laboring to get rid of the Missouri Compromise. Their motive was to defend slavery and
especially to forestall a successful movement for
emancipation in the State of Missouri.

From early in January, 1854, until late in May,
Douglas's Nebraska bill held the attention of
Congress and of the entire country. At first the
measure simply assumed that the Missouri Compromise had been superseded by the Act of 1850.
Later the bill was amended in such a way as to
repeal distinctly that time-honored act. At first
the plan was to organize Nebraska as a single
Territory extending from Texas to Canada. Later
it was proposed to organize separate Territories,
one west of Missouri under the name of Kansas,
the other west of Iowa under the name of Nebraska.
Opposition came from Free-soilers, from Northern
Whigs and a few Whigs from the South, and from a
large proportion of Northern Democrats. The
repeal of the Missouri Compromise came like a
thunderbolt out of a clear sky to the people of the
North. For a time Douglas was the most unpopu-
lar of political leaders and was apparently repudiated by his party. The first name designating
the opponents of the Douglas bill was "Anti-

Nebraska men," for which the name Republican was gradually substituted and in 1856 became the accepted title of the party.

The provision for two territorial governments instead of one carried with it the idea of a continued balance between slave and free States; Kansas, being on a geographical parallel with the slave States, would probably permit slavery, while Nebraska would be occupied by free-state immigrants. Though this was a commonly accepted view, Eli Thayer of Worcester, Massachusetts, and a few others took a different view. They proposed to make an end of the discussion of the extension of slavery by sending free men who were opposed to slavery to occupy the territory open for settlement. To attain this object they organized an Emigrant Aid Company incorporated under the laws of the State. Even before the bill was passed, the corporation was in full working order. Thayer himself traveled extensively throughout the Northern States stimulating interest in western emigration, with the conviction that the disturbing question could be peacefully settled in this way. California had thus been saved to freedom; why not all other Territories? The new company had as adviser and colaborer

Dr. Charles Robinson, who had crossed the Kansas
Territory on his way to California and had acquired
valuable experience in the art of state-building
under peculiar conditions.

The first party sent out by the Emigrant Aid
Company arrived in Kansas early in August, 1854,
and selected the site for the town of Lawrence.
During the later months of the year, four other
parties were sent out, in all numbering nearly
seven hundred. Through extensive advertise-
ment by the company, through the general interest
in the subject and the natural flow of emigration
to the West, Kansas was receiving large accessions
of free-state settlers.

Meanwhile the men of Missouri, some of whom
had striven for a decade to secure the privilege of
extending slavery into the new Territory, were not
idle. Instantly upon the removal of legal barriers, they occupied adjacent lands, founded towns,
staked out claims, formed plans for preëmpting the
entire region and for forestalling or driving out all
intruders. They had at first the advantage of
position, for they did not find it difficult to maintain two homes, one in Kansas for purposes of
voting and fighting and another in Missouri for
actual residence.

Andrew H. Reeder, a Pennsylvania Democrat of strong pro-slavery prejudices, was appointed first Governor of the Territory. When he arrived in Kansas in October, 1854, there were already several thousand settlers on the ground and others were continually arriving. He appointed the 29th of November for the election of a delegate to Congress. On that day several hundred Missourians came into the Territory and voted. There was no violence and no contest; the free-state men had no separate candidate. Notwithstanding the violence of language used by opposing factions, notwithstanding the organization of secret societies pledged to drive out all Northern intruders, there was no serious disturbance until March 30, 1855, the day appointed for the election of members of the territorial Legislature. On that day the Missourians came full five thousand strong, armed with guns, bowie-knives, and revolvers. They met with no resistance from the residents, who were unarmed. They took charge of the precincts and chose pro-slavery delegates with one exception. Governor Reeder protested and recommended to the precincts the filing of protests. Only seven responded, however, and in these cases new elections were held and contesting delegates elected

The Governor issued certificates to these and to all those who in other precincts had been chosen by the horde from Missouri. When the Legislature met in July, the seven contests were decided in favor of the pro-slavery party, the single free-state member resigned, and the assembly was unanimous.

Governor Reeder fully expected that President Pierce would nullify the election, and to this end he made a journey to Washington in April. On the way he delivered a public address at Easton, Pennsylvania, describing in lurid colors the outrage which had been perpetrated upon the people of Kansas by the "border ruffians" from Missouri, and asserting that the accounts in the Northern press had not been exaggerated.

While Governor Reeder in contact with the actual events in Kansas was becoming an active Free-soiler, President Pierce in association with Jefferson Davis and others of his party was developing active sympathies with the people of western Missouri. To the President this invasion of territory west of the slave State by Northern men aided by Northern corporations seemed a violation of the Kansas-Nebraska Act, and he sought to induce Reeder to resign. This, however,

the Governor positively refused to do unless the
President would formally approve his conduct in
Kansas — an endorsement which required more
fortitude than President Pierce possessed. On his
return to Kansas, determined to do what he could
to protect the Kansas people from injustice, he
called the Legislature to meet at Pawnee, a point
far removed from the Missouri border. Immediately upon their organization at that place the
members of the Legislature adjourned to meet at
Shawnee, near the border of Missouri. The Governor, who decided that this action was illegal, then
refused to recognize the Assembly at the new place.
A deadlock thus ensued which was broken on the
15th of August by the removal of Governor Reeder
and the appointment of Wilson Shannon of Ohio
in his place.

In the meantime the territorial Legislature had
adjourned, having "enacted" an elaborate pro-
slavery code made up from the slave code of Missouri with a number of special adaptations. For
example, it was made a penitentiary offense to
deny by speaking or writing, or by printing, or by
introducing any printed matter, the right of persons to hold slaves in the Territory; no man was
eligible to jury service who was conscientiously

opposed to holding slaves; and lawyers were bound
by oath to support the territorial statutes.

The free-state men, with the approval of Reeder,
refused to recognize the Legislature and inaugurated a movement in the fall of 1855 to adopt a constitution and to organize a provisional territorial
Government preparatory to admission as a State,
following in this respect the procedure in California and Michigan. A convention met in Topeka
in October, 1855, and completed on the 11th of
November the draft of a constitution which prohibited slavery. On the 15th of December the
constitution was approved by a practically unanimous vote, only free-state men taking part
in the election. A month later a Legislature was
elected and at the same time Charles Robinson
was elected Governor of the new commonwealth.
In the previous October, Reeder had been chosen
Free-soil delegate to Congress. The Topeka free-
state Legislature met on the 4th of March, 1856,
and after petitioning Congress to admit Kansas
under the Topeka constitution, adjourned until
the 4th of July pending the action of Congress.
Thus at the end of two years two distinct Governments had come into existence within the Territory
of Kansas.

It speaks volumes for the self-control and moderation of the two parties that no hostile encounter had occurred between the contestants. When the armed Missourians came in March, 1855, the unarmed settlers offered no resistance. Afterward, however, they supplied themselves with Sharp's rifles and organized a militia. With the advent of Governor Shannon in September, 1855, the pro-slavery position was much strengthened. In November, in a quarrel over a land claim, a free-state settler by the name of Dow was killed. The murderer escaped, but a friend of the victim was accused of uttering threats against a friend of the murderer. For this offense a posse led by Sheriff Jones, a Missourian, seized him, and would have carried him away if fourteen free-state men had not "persuaded" the Sheriff to surrender his prisoner. This interference was accepted by the Missourians as a signal for battle. The rescuers must be arrested and punished. A large force of infuriated Missourians and pro-slavery settlers assembled for a raid upon the town of Lawrence. In the meantime the Lawrence militia planned and executed a systematic defense of the town. When the two armies came within speaking distance, a parley ensued in which the Governor took a leading part in settling the affair without a hostile shot. This is known in Kansas history as the "Wakarusa War."

The progress of affairs in Kansas was followed with intense interest in all parts of the country. North and South vied with each other in the encouragement of emigration to Kansas. Colonel Buford of Alabama sold a large number of slaves and devoted the proceeds to meeting the expense of conducting a troop of three hundred men to Kansas in the winter of 1856. They went armed with "the sword of the spirit," and all provided with Bibles supplied by the leading churches. Arrived in the territory, they were duly furnished with more worldly weapons and were drilled for action. About the same time a parallel incident is said to have occurred in New Haven, Connecticut. A deacon in one of the churches had enlisted a company of seventy bound for Kansas. A meeting was held in the church to raise money to defray expenses. The leader of the company declared that they also needed rifles for self-defense. Forthwith Professor Silliman, of the University, subscribed one Sharp's rifle, and others followed with like pledges. Finally Henry Ward Beecher, who was the speaker of the occasion, rose and promised that, if twenty-five rifles were pledged on the spot, Plymouth Church in Brooklyn would be responsible for the remaining twenty-five that were needed. He had already said in a previous address that for the slaveholders of Kansas, Sharp's rifles were a greater moral agency than the Bible. This led to the designation of the weapons as "Beecher's Bibles." Such was the spirit which prevailed in the two sections of the country.

President Pierce had now become intensely hostile towards the free-state inhabitants of Kansas. Having recognized the Legislature elected on March 30, 1855, as the legitimate Government, he sent a special message to Congress on January 24, 1856, in which he characterized as revolutionary the movement of the free-state men to organize a separate Government in Kansas. From the President's point of view, the emissaries of the New England Emigrant Aid Association were unlawful invaders. In this position he not only had the support of the South, but was powerfully seconded by Stephen A. Douglas and other Northern Democrats.

The attitude of the Administration at Washington was a source of great encouragement to Sheriff Jones and his associates, who were anxious to wreak their vengeance on the city of Lawrence for

the outcome of the Wakarusa War. Jones came
to Lawrence apparently for the express purpose of
picking a quarrel, for he revived the old dispute
about the rescuing party of the previous fall. As a
consequence one enraged opponent slapped him in
the face, and at last an unknown assassin entered
the sheriff's tent by night and inflicted a revolver
wound in his back. Though the citizens of Lawrence were greatly chagrined at this event and
offered a reward for the discovery of the assailant,
the attack upon the sheriff was made the signal for
drastic procedure against the town of Lawrence.
A grand jury found indictments for treason against
Reeder, Robinson, and other leading citizens of
the town. The United States marshal gave notice
that he expected resistance in making arrests and
called upon all law-abiding citizens of the Territory to aid in executing the law. It was a welcome
summons to the pro-slavery forces. Not only local
militia companies responded but also Buford's
company and various companies from Missouri,
in all more than seven hundred men, with two
cannon. It had always been the set purpose of the
free-state men not to resist federal authority by
force, unless as a last resort, and they had no intention of opposing the marshal in making arrests.

He performed his duty without hindrance and then placed the armed troops under the command of Sheriff Jones, who proceeded first to destroy the printing-press of the town of Lawrence. Then, against the protest of the marshal and Colonel Buford, the vindictive sheriff trained his guns upon the new hotel which was the pride of the city; the ruin of the building was made complete by fire, while a drunken mob pillaged the town.

On May 22, 1856, the day following the attack upon Lawrence, Charles Sumner was struck down in the United States Senate on account of a speech made in defense of the rights of Kansas settlers. The two events, which were reported at the same time in the daily press, furnished the key-note to the presidential campaign of that year, for nominating conventions followed in a few days and "bleeding Kansas" was the all-absorbing issue. In spite of the destruction of property in Lawrence and the arrest of the leaders of the free-state party, Kansas had not been plunged into a state of civil war. The free-state party had fired no hostile shot. Governor Robinson and his associates still relied upon public opinion and they accepted the wanton attack upon Lawrence as the best assurance that they would yet win their cause by legal means.

A change, however, soon took place which is associated with the entrance of John Brown into the history of Kansas. Brown and his sons were living at Osawatomie, some thirty miles south of Lawrence. They were present at the Wakarusa War in December, 1855, and were on their way to the defense of Lawrence on May 21, 1856, when they were informed that the town had been destroyed. Three days after this event Brown and his sons with two or three others made a midnight raid upon their pro-slavery neighbors living in the Pottawatomie valley and slew five men. The authors of this deed were not certainly known until the publication of a confession of one of the party in 1879, twenty years after the chief actor had won the reputation of a martyr to the cause of liberty. The Browns, however, were suspected at the time; warrants were out for their arrest; and their homes were destroyed.

For more than three months after this incident, Kansas was in a state of war; in fact, two distinct varieties of warfare were carried on. Publicly organized companies on both sides engaged in acts of attack and defense, while at the same time irresponsible secret bands were busy in violent reprisals, in plunder and assassination. In both of these forms of warfare, the free-state men proved themselves fully equal to their opponents, and Governor Shannon was entirely unable to cope with the situation. It is estimated that two hundred men were slain and two million dollars' worth of property was destroyed.

The state of affairs in Kansas served to win many Northern Democrats to the support of the Republicans. The Administration at Washington was held responsible for the violence and bloodshed. The Democratic leaders in the political campaign, determined now upon a complete change in the Government of the Territory, appointed J. W. Geary as Governor and placed General Smith in charge of the troops. The new incumbents, both from Pennsylvania, entered upon their labors early in September, and before the October state elections Geary was able to report that peace reigned throughout the Territory. A prompt reaction in favor of the Democrats followed. Buchanan, their presidential candidate, rejoiced in the fact that order had been restored by two citizens of his own State. It was now very generally conceded that Kansas would become a free State, and intimate associates of Buchanan assured the public that he was himself of that opinion and that if

elected he would insure to the free-state party
even-handed justice. Thousands of voters were
thus won to Buchanan's support. There was a
general distrust of the Republican candidate as
a man lacking political experience, and a strong
conservative reaction against the idea of electing
a President by the votes of only one section of the
country. At the election in November, Buchanan
received a majority of sixty of the electoral votes
over Frémont, but in the popular vote he fell short
of a majority by nearly 400,000. Fillmore, candidate of the Whig and the American parties, received 874,000 votes.

There was still profound distrust of the administration of the Territory of Kansas, and the free-
state settlers refused to vote at the election set
for the choosing of a new territorial Legislature
in October. The result was another pro-slavery
assembly. Governor Geary, however, determined
to secure and enforce just treatment of both parties.
He was at once brought into violent conflict with
the Legislature in an experience which was almost
an exact counterpart of that of Governor Reeder;
and Washington did not support his efforts to secure fair dealings. A pro-slavery deputation visited
President Pierce in February, 1857, and returned

with the assurance that Governor Geary would be removed. Without waiting for the President to act, Geary resigned in disgust on the 4th of March. Of the three Governors whom President Pierce appointed, two became active supporters of the free-state party and a third, Governor Shannon, fled from the territory in mortal terror lest he should be slain by members of the party which he had tried to serve.

CHAPTER XI

CHARLES SUMNER

THE real successor to John Quincy Adams as the protagonist of the anti-slavery cause in Congress proved to be not Seward but Charles Sumner of Massachusetts. This newcomer entered the Senate without previous legislative experience but with an unusual equipment for the rôle he was to play. A graduate of Harvard College at the age of nineteen, he had entered upon the study of law in the newly organized law school in which Joseph Story held one of the two professorships. He was admitted to the bar in 1834, but three years later he left his slender law practice for a long period of European travel. This three years' sojourn brought him into intimate touch with the leading spirits in arts, letters, and public life in England and on the Continent, and thus ripened his talents to their full maturity. He returned to his law practice poor in pocket but rich in the possession of lifelong friendships and happy memories.

Sumner's political career did not begin until 1847, when as a Whig he not only opposed any further extension of slavery but strove to commit his party to the policy of emancipation in all the States. Failing in this attempt, Sumner became an active Free-soiler in 1848. He was twice a candidate for Congress on the Free-soil ticket but failed of election. In 1851 he was elected to the United States Senate by a coalition between his party and the Democrats. This is the only public office he ever held, but he was continuously re-elected until his death in 1874.

John Quincy Adams had addressed audiences trained in the old school, which did not defend slavery on moral grounds. Charles Sumner faced audiences of the new school, which upheld the institution as a righteous moral order. This explains the chief difference in the attitude of the two leaders. Sumner, like Adams, began as an opponent of pro-slavery aggression, but he went farther: he attacked the institution itself as a great moral evil.

As a constitutional lawyer Sumner is not the equal of his predecessor, Daniel Webster. He is

less original, less convincing in the enunciation of
broad general principles. He appears rather as
a special pleader marshaling all available forces
against the one institution which assailed the
Union. In this particular work, he surpassed all
others, for, with his unbounded industry, he permitted no precedent, no legal advantage, no incident of history, no fact in current politics fitted to
strengthen his cause, to escape his untiring search.
He showed a marvelous skill in the selection, arrangement, and presentation of his materials, and
for his models he took the highest forms of classic
forensic utterance.

Sumner exhibited the ordinary aloofness and
lack of familiarity with actual conditions in the
South which was characteristic of the New England
abolitionist. He perceived no race problem, no
peculiar difficulty in the readjustments of master
and slave which were involved in emancipation,
and he ignored all obstacles to the accomplishment
of his ends. Webster's arraignment of South Carolina was directed against an alleged erroneous
dogma and only incidentally affected personal
morality. The reaction, therefore, was void of
bitter resentment. Sumner's charges were directed
against alleged moral turpitude, and the classic

form and scrupulous regard for parliamentary
rules which he observed only added to the feeling
of personal resentment on the part of his opponents. Some of the defenders of slavery were themselves devoted students of the classics, but they
found that the orations of Demosthenes furnished
nothing suited to their purpose. The result was a
humiliating exhibition of weakness, personal abuse,
and vindictiveness on their part.

There was a conspiracy of silence on the slavery
question in 1852. Each of the national parties
was definitely committed to the support of the
compromise and especially to the faithful observ-
ance of the Fugitive Slave Law. Free-soilers had
distinctly declined in numbers and influence during the four preceding years. Only a handful of
members in each House of Congress remained un-
affiliated with the parties whose platforms had ordained silence on the one issue of chief public concern. It was by a mere accident in Massachusetts
politics that Charles Sumner was sent to the Senate
as a man free on all public questions.

While the parties were making their nominations
for the Presidency, Sumner sought diligently for
an opportunity in the Senate to give utterance to
the sentiments of his party on the repeal of the

Fugitive Slave Act. But not until late in August did he overcome the resistance of the combined opposition and gain the floor. The watchmen were caught off guard when Sumner introduced an amendment to an appropriation bill which enabled him to deliver a carefully prepared address, several hours in length, calling for the repeal of the law.

The first part of this speech is devoted to the general topic of the relation of the national Government to slavery and was made in answer to the demand of Calhoun and his followers for the direct national recognition of slavery. For such a demand Sumner found no warrant. By the decision of Lord Mansfield, said he, "the state of slavery" was declared to be "of such a nature, that it is incapable of being introduced on any reasons, moral or political, but *only by positive law.* . . . it is so odious, that nothing can be suffered to support it but positive law." Adopting the same principle, the Supreme Court of the State of Mississippi, a tribunal of slaveholders, asserted that "slavery is condemned by reason and the Laws of Nature. It exists, and can *only* exist, through municipal regulations." So also declared the Supreme Court of Kentucky and numerous other tribunals. This aspect of the subject furnished Sumner occasion

for a masterly array of all the utterances in favor
of liberty to be found in the Constitution, in the
Declaration of Independence, in the constitutional
conventions, in the principles of common law. All
these led up to and supported the one grand conclusion that, when Washington took the oath as
President of the United States, "slavery existed
nowhere on the national territory" and therefore
"is in no respect a national institution." Apply
the principles of the Constitution in their purity,
then, and "in all national territories slavery will
be impossible. On the high seas, under the national flag, slavery will be impossible. In the
District of Columbia, slavery will instantly cease.
Inspired by these principles, Congress can give
no sanction to slavery by the admission of new
slave States. Nowhere under the Constitution can
the Nation by legislation or otherwise, support
slavery, hunt slaves, or hold property in man.
. . . As slavery is banished from the national
jurisdiction, it will cease to vex our national politics. It may linger in the States as a local institution; but it will no longer engender national
animosities when it no longer demands national
support."

The second part of Sumner's address dealt

directly with the Fugitive Slave Act of 1850. It is much less convincing and suggests more of the characteristics of the special pleader with a difficult case. Sumner here undertook to prove that Congress exceeded its powers when it presumed to lay down rules for the rendition of fugitive slaves, and this task exceeded even his power as a constitutional lawyer.

The circumstances under which Sumner attacked slavery were such as to have alarmed a less self-centered man, for the two years following the introduction of the Nebraska bill were marked by the most acrimonious debate in the history of Congress, and by physical encounters, challenges, and threats of violence. But though Congressmen carried concealed weapons, Sumner went his way unarmed and apparently in complete unconcern as to any personal danger, though it is known that he was fully aware that in the faithful performance of what he deemed to be his duty he was incurring the risk of assassination.

The pro-slavery party manifested on all occasions a disposition to make the most of the weak point in Sumner's constitutional argument against the Fugitive Slave Law. He was accused of taking an oath to support the Constitution though at the same time intending to violate one of its provisions. In a discussion, in June, 1854, over a petition praying for the repeal of the Fugitive Slave Act, Senator Butler of South Carolina put the question directly to Senator Sumner whether he would himself unite with others in returning a fugitive to his master.   Sumner's quick reply was, "Is thy servant a dog that he should do this thing?"   Enraged Southerners followed this remark with a most bitter onslaught upon Sumner which lasted for two days.   When Sumner again got the floor, he said in reference to Senator Butler's remark: "In fitful phrase, which seemed to come from unconscious excitement, so common with the Senator, he shot forth various cries about 'dogs,' and, among other things, asked if there was any 'dog' in the Constitution?   The Senator did not seem to bear in mind, through the heady currents of that moment that, by the false interpretation he fastens upon the Constitution, he has helped to nurture there a whole kennel of Carolina bloodhounds, trained, with savage jaw and insatiable in scent, for the hunt of flying bondmen.   No, sir, I do not believe that there is any 'kennel of bloodhounds,' or even any 'dog' in the Constitution."   Thereafter offensive personal references between the Senators from Massachusetts and South Carolina became habitual. These personalities were a source of regret to many of Sumner's best friends, but they fill a small place, after all, in his great work. Nor were they the chief source of rancor on the part of his enemies, for Southern orators were accustomed to personalities in debate. Sumner was feared and hated principally because his presence in Congress endangered the institution of slavery.

Sumner's speech on the crime against Kansas was perhaps the most remarkable effort of his career. It had been known for many weeks that Sumner was preparing to speak upon the burning question, and his friends had already expressed anxiety for his personal safety. For the larger part of two days, May 19 and 20, 1856, he held the reluctant attention of the Senate. For the delivery of this speech he chose a time which was most opportune. The crime against Kansas had, in a sense, culminated in March of the previous year, but the settlers had refused to submit to the Government set up by hostile invaders. They had armed themselves for the defense of their rights, had elected a Governor and a Legislature by voluntary association, had called a convention, and had adopted a constitution preparatory to admission to the Union.   That constitution was now before the Senate for approval.   President Pierce, Stephen A. Douglas, and all the Southern leaders had decided to treat as treasonable acts the efforts of Kansas settlers to secure an orderly government. Their plans for the arrest of the leaders were well advanced and the arrests were actually made on the day after Sumner had concluded his speech.

A paragraph in the address is prophetic of what occurred within a week.   Douglas had introduced a bill recognizing the Legislature chosen by the Missourians as the legal Government and providing for the formation of a constitution under its initiative at some future date.   After describing this proposed action as a continuation of the crime against Kansas, Sumner declared: "Sir, you cannot expect that the people of Kansas will submit to the usurpation which this bill sets up and bids them bow before, as the Austrian tyrant set up the ducal hat in the Swiss market-place.   If you madly persevere, Kansas will not be without her William Tell, who will refuse at all hazards to recognize the tyrannical edict; and this will be the beginning of civil war."

To keep historical sequence clear at this point, all thought of John Brown should be eliminated, for he was then unknown to the public. It must be remembered that Governor Robinson and the free-state settlers were, as Sumner probably knew, prepared to resist the general Government as soon as there should be a clear case of outrage for which the Administration at Washington could be held directly responsible. Such a case occurred when the United States marshal placed federal troops in the hands of Sheriff Jones to assist in looting the town of Lawrence. Governor Robinson no longer had any scruples in advising forcible resistance to all who used force to impose upon Kansas a Government which the people had rejected.

In the course of his address Sumner compared Senators Butler and Douglas to Don Quixote and Sancho Panza, saying: "The Senator from South Carolina has read many books of chivalry, and believes himself a chivalrous knight, with sentiments of honor and courage. Of course he has chosen a mistress to whom he has made his vows, and who, though ugly to others, is always lovely to him; though polluted in the sight of the world, is chaste in his sight. I mean the harlot Slavery. Let her be impeached in character, or any proposition be made to shut her out from the extension of her wantonness, and no extravagance of manner or hardihood of assertion is then too great for the Senator."

When Sumner concluded, the gathering storm broke forth. Cass of Michigan, after saying that he had listened to the address with equal surprise and regret, characterized it as "the most un-American and unpatriotic that ever grated on the ears of the members of that high body." Douglas and Mason were personal and abusive. Douglas, recalling Sumner's answer to Senator Butler's question whether he would assist in returning a slave, renewed the charge made two years earlier that Sumner had violated his oath of office. This attack called forth from Sumner another attempt to defend the one weak point in his speech of 1852, for he was always irritated by reference to this subject, and at the same time he enjoyed a fine facility in the use of language which irritated others.

One utterance in Douglas's reply to Sumner is of special significance in view of what occurred two days later: "Is it his object to provoke some of us to kick him as we would a dog in the street, that he may get sympathy upon the just chastisement?" Two days later Sumner was sitting alone at his desk in the Senate chamber after adjournment when Preston Brooks, a nephew of Senator Butler and a member of the lower House, entered and accosted him with the statement that he had read Sumner's speech twice and that it was a libel on South Carolina and upon a kinsman of his. Thereupon Brooks followed his words by striking Sumner on the head with a cane. Though the Senator was dazed and blinded by the unexpected attack, his assailant rained blow after blow until he had broken the cane and Sumner lay prostrate and bleeding at his feet. Brooks's remarks in the House of Representatives almost a month after the event leave no doubt of his determination to commit murder had he failed to overcome his antagonist with a cane. He had also taken the precaution to have two of his friends ready to prevent any interference before the punishment was completed. Toombs of Georgia witnessed a part of the assault and expressed approval of the act, and everywhere throughout the South, in the public press, in legislative halls, in public meetings, Brooks was hailed as a hero. The resolution for his expulsion introduced in the House received the support of only one vote from south of Mason and Dixon's Line. A large majority favored the resolution, but not the required two-thirds majority. Brooks, however, thought best to resign but was triumphantly returned to his seat with only six votes against him. Nothing was left undone to express Southern gratitude, and he received gifts of canes innumerable as symbols of his valor. Yet before his death, which occurred in the following January, he confessed to his friend Orr that he was sick of being regarded as the representative of bullies and disgusted at receiving testimonials of their esteem.

With similar unanimity the North condemned and resented the assault that had been made upon Sumner. From party considerations, if for no other reasons, Democrats regretted the event. Republicans saw in the brutal attack and in the manner of its reception in the South another evidence of the irrepressible conflict between slavery and freedom. They were ready to take up the issue so forcibly presented by their fallen leader. A part of the regular order of exercises at public meetings of Republicans was to express sympathy with their wounded champion and with the Kansas people of the pillaged town of Lawrence, and to adopt ways and means to bring to an end the Administration which they held responsible for these outrages. Sumner, though silenced, was eloquent in a new and more effective way. A half million copies of *The Crime against Kansas* were printed and circulated. On the issue thus presented, Northern Democrats became convinced that their defeat at the pending election was certain, and their leaders instituted the change in their program which has been described in a previous chapter. They had made an end of the war in Kansas and drew from their candidate for the Presidency the assurance that just treatment should at last be meted out to harassed Kansas.

Though Sumner's injuries were at first regarded as slight, they eventually proved to be extremely serious. After two attempts to resume his place in the Senate, he found that he was unable to remain; yet when his term expired, he was almost unanimously reëlected. Much of his time for three and a half years he spent in Europe. In December, 1859, he seemed sufficiently recovered to resume senatorial duties, but it was not until the following June that he again addressed the Senate. On that occasion he delivered his last great philippic against slavery. The subject under discussion was still the admission of Kansas as a free State, and, as he remarked in his opening sentences, he resumed the discussion precisely where he had left off more than four years before.

Sumner had assumed the task of uttering a final

word against slavery as barbarism and a barrier
to civilization. He spoke under the impelling
power of a conviction in his God-given mission to
utilize a great occasion to the full and for a noble
end. For this work his whole life had been a preparation. Accustomed from early youth to spend
ten hours a day with books on law, history, and
classic literature, he knew as no other man then
knew what aid the past could offer to the struggle
for freedom. The bludgeon of the would-be assassin had not impaired his memory, and four years of
enforced leisure enabled him to fulfill his highest
ideals of perfect oratorical form. Personalities he
eliminated from this final address, and blemishes
he pruned away. In his earlier speeches he had
been limited by the demands of the particular question under discussion, but in *The Barbarism of
Slavery* he was free to deal with the general subject,
and he utilized incidents in American slavery to
demonstrate the general upward trend of history.
The orator was sustained by the full consciousness
that his utterances were in harmony with the
grand sweep of historic truth as well as with the
spirit of the present age.

Sumner was not a party man and was at no time
in complete harmony with his coworkers. It was

always a question whether his speeches had a favorable effect upon the immediate action of Congress; there can, however, be no doubt of the fact that the larger public was edified and influenced. Copies of *The Crime against Kansas* and *The Barbarism of Slavery* were printed and circulated by the million and were eagerly read from beginning to end. They gave final form to the thoughts and utterances of many political leaders both in America and in Europe. More than any other man it was Charles Sumner who, with a wealth of historical learning and great skill in forensic art, put the irrepressible conflict between slavery and freedom in its proper setting in human history.

CHAPTER XII

KANSAS AND BUCHANAN

In view of the presidential election of 1856 Northern Democrats entertained no doubts that Kansas, now occupied by a majority of free-state men, would be received as a free State without further ado. The case was different with the Democrats of western Missouri, already for ten years in close touch with those Southern leaders who were determined either to secure new safeguards for slavery or to form an independent confederacy. Their program was to continue their efforts to make Kansas a slave State or at least to maintain the disturbance there until the conditions appeared favorable for secession.

In February, 1857, the pro-slavery territorial Legislature provided for the election of delegates to a constitutional convention, but Governor Geary vetoed the act because no provision was made for submitting the proposed constitution to the vote of the people. The bill was passed over his veto, and arrangements were made for registration which free-state men regarded as imperfect, inadequate, or fraudulent.

President Buchanan undoubtedly intended to do full justice to the people of Kansas. To this end he chose Robert J. Walker, a Mississippi Democrat, as Governor of Kansas. Walker was a statesman of high rank, who had been associated with Buchanan in the Cabinet of James K. Polk. Three times he refused to accept the office and finally undertook the mission only from a sense of duty. Being aware of the fate of Governor Geary, Walker insisted on an explicit understanding with Buchanan that his policies should not be repudiated by the federal Administration. Late in May he went to Kansas with high hopes and expectations. But the free-state party had persisted in the repudiation of a Government which had been first set up by an invading army and, as they alleged, had since then been perpetuated by fraud. They had absolutely refused to take part in any election called by that Government and had continued to keep alive their own legislative assembly. Despite Walker's efforts to persuade them to take part in the election of delegates to the constitutional convention, they resolutely held aloof. Yet, as they became convinced that he was acting in good faith, they did participate in the October elections to the territorial Legislature, electing nine out of the thirteen councilors and twenty-four out of the thirty-nine representatives. Gross frauds had been perpetrated in two districts, and the Governor made good his promise by rejecting the fraudulent votes. In one case a poll list had been made up by copying an old Cincinnati register.

In the meantime, thanks to the abstention of the free-state people, the pro-slavery party had secured absolute control of the constitutional convention. Yet there was the most absolute assurance by the Governor in the name of the President of the United States that no constitution would be sent to Congress for approval which had not received the sanction of a majority of the voters of the Territory. This was Walker's reiterated promise, and President Buchanan had on this point been equally explicit.

When, therefore, the pro-slavery constitutional convention met at Lecompton in October, Kansas had a free-state Legislature duly elected. To make Kansas still a slave State it was necessary to get rid of that Legislature and of the Governor through

whose agency it had been chosen, and at the same
time to frame a constitution which would secure
the approval of the Buchanan Administration.
Incredible as it may seem, all this was actually
accomplished.

John Calhoun, who had been chosen president
of the Lecompton convention, spent some time in
Washington before the adjourned meeting of the
convention. He secured the aid of master-hands
at manipulation. Walker had already been dis-
credited at the White House on account of his
rejection of fraudulent returns at the October
election of members to the Legislature. The convention was unwilling to take further chances on a
matter of that sort, and it consequently made it a
part of the constitution that the president of the
convention should have entire charge of the election to be held for its approval. The free-state
Legislature was disposed of by placing in the constitution a provision that all existing laws should
remain in force until the election of a Legislature
provided for under the constitution.

The master-stroke of the convention, however,
was the provision for submitting the constitution
to the vote of the people. Voters were not permitted to accept or reject the instrument; all votes

were to be for the constitution either "with slavery" or "with no slavery." But the document itself recognized slavery as already existing and declared the right of slave property like other property "before and higher than any constitutional sanction." Other provisions made emancipation difficult by providing in any case for complete monetary remuneration and for the consent of the owners. There were numerous other provisions offensive to free-state men. It had been rightly surmised that they would take no part in such an election and that "the constitution with slavery" would be approved. The vote on the constitution was set for the 21st of December. For the constitution with slavery 6226 votes were recorded and 569 for the constitution without slavery.

While these events were taking place, Walker went to Washington to enter his protest but resigned after finding only a hostile reception by the President and his Cabinet. Stanton, who was acting Governor in the absence of Walker, then called together the free-state Legislature, which set January 4, 1858, as the date for approving or rejecting the Lecompton Constitution. At this election the votes cast were 138 for the constitution with slavery, 24 for the constitution without slavery, and 10,226 against the constitution. But President Buchanan had become thoroughly committed to the support of the Lecompton Constitution. Disregarding the advice of the new Governor, he sent the Lecompton Constitution to Congress with the recommendation that Kansas be admitted to the Union as a slave State.

Here was a crisis big with the fate of the Democratic party, if not of the Union. Stephen A. Douglas had already given notice that he would oppose the Lecompton Constitution. In favor of its rejection he made a notable speech which called forth the bitterest enmity from the South and arrayed all the forces of the Administration against him. Supporters of Douglas were removed from office, and anti-Douglas men were put in their places. In his fight against the fraudulent constitution Douglas himself, however, still had the support of a majority of Northern Democrats, especially in the Western States, and that of all the Republicans in Congress. A bill to admit Kansas passed the Senate, but in the House a proviso was attached requiring that the constitution should first be submitted to the people of Kansas for acceptance or rejection. This amendment was finally accepted by the Senate with the modification that, if the people voted for the constitution, the State should have a large donation of public land, but that if they rejected it, they should not be admitted as a State until they had a population large enough to entitle them to a representative in the lower House. The vote of the people was cast on August 2, 1858, and the constitution was finally rejected by a majority of nearly twelve thousand. Thus resulted the last effort to impose slavery on the people of Kansas.

Although the war between slavery and freedom was fought out in miniature in Kansas, the immediate issue was the preservation of slavery in Missouri. This, however, involved directly the prospect of emancipation in other border States and ultimate complete emancipation in all the States. The issue is well stated in a Fourth of July address which Charles Robinson delivered at Lawrence, Kansas, in 1855, after the invasion of Missourians to influence the March election of that year, but before the beginning of bloody conflict:

What reason is given for the cowardly invasion of our rights by our neighbors? They say that if Kansas is allowed to be free the institution of slavery in their own State will be in danger. . . .   If the people of Missouri make it necessary, by their unlawful course, for us to establish freedom in that State in order to enjoy the liberty of governing ourselves in Kansas, then let that be the issue. If Kansas and the whole North must be enslaved, or Missouri become free, then let her be made free. Aye! and if to be free ourselves, slavery must be abolished in the whole country, then let us accept that issue. If black slavery in a part of the States is incompatible with white freedom in any State, then let black slavery be abolished from all. As men espousing the principles of the Declaration of the Fathers, we can do nothing else than accept these issues.

The men who saved Kansas to freedom were not abolitionists in the restricted sense. Governor Walker found in 1857 that a considerable majority of the free-state men were Democrats and that some were from the South. Nearly all actual settlers, from whatever source they came, were free-state men who felt that a slave was a burden in such a country as Kansas. For example, during the first winter of the occupation of Kansas, an owner of nineteen slaves was himself forced to work like a trooper to keep them from freezing; and, indeed, one of them did freeze to death and another was seriously injured.

In spite of all the advertising of opportunity and all the pressure brought to bear upon Southerners to settle in Kansas, at no time did the number of slaves in the Territory reach three hundred. The climate and the soil made for freedom, and the Governors were not the only persons who were converted to free-state principles by residence in the Territory.

CHAPTER XIII

THE SUPREME COURT IN POLITICS

THE decision and arguments of the Supreme Court upon the Dred Scott case were published on March 6, 1857, two days after the inauguration of President Buchanan. The decision had been agreed upon many months before, and the appeal of the negro, Dred Scott, had been decided by rulings which in no way involved the validity of the Missouri Compromise. Nevertheless, a majority of the judges determined to give to the newly developed theory of John C. Calhoun the appearance of the sanctity of law. According to Chief Justice Taney's dictum, those who made the Constitution gave to those clauses defining the power of Congress over the Territories an erroneous meaning. On numerous occasions Congress had by statute excluded slavery from the public domain. This, in the judgment of the Chief Justice, they had no right to do, and such legislation was unconstitutional and void. Specifically the Missouri Compromise had never had any binding force as law. Property in slaves was as sacred as property in any other form, and slave-owners had equal claim with other property owners to protection in all the Territories of the United States. Neither Congress nor a territorial Legislature could infringe such equal rights.

According to popular understanding, the Supreme Court declared "that the negro has no rights which the white man is bound to respect." But Chief Justice Taney did not use these words merely as an expression of his own or of the Court's opinion. He used them in a way much more contemptible and inexcusable to the minds of men of strong anti-slavery convictions. He put them into the mouths of the fathers of the Republic, who wrote the Declaration of Independence, framed the Constitution, organized state Governments, and gave to negroes full rights of citizenship, including the right to vote. But how explain this strange inconsistency? The Chief Justice was equal to the occasion. He insisted that in recent years there had come about a better understanding of the phraseology of the Declaration of Independence. The words, "All men are created equal," he admitted "would seem to embrace the whole human family, and if they were used in a similar instrument at this day they would be so understood." But the writers of that instrument had not, he said, intended to include men of the African race, who were at that time regarded as not forming any part of the people. Therefore — strange logic! — these men of the revolutionary era who treated negroes actually as citizens having full equal rights did not understand the meaning of their own words, which could be comprehended only after three-quarters of a century when, forsooth, equal rights had been denied to all persons of African descent.

The ruling of the Court in the Dred Scott case came at a time when Northern people had a better idea of the spirit and teachings of the founders of the Republic regarding the slavery question than any generation before or since has had. The campaign that had just closed had been characterized by a high order of discussion, and it was also emphatically a reading campaign. The new Republican party planted itself squarely on the principles enunciated by Thomas Jefferson, the reputed founder of the old Republican party. They went back to the policy of the fathers, whose words on the subject of slavery they eagerly read. From this source also came the chief material for their public addresses. To the common man who was thus indoctrinated, the Chief Justice, in describing the sentiments of the fathers respecting slavery, appeared to be doing what Horace Greeley was wont to describe as "saying a thing and being conscious while saying it that the thing is not true."

The Dred Scott decision laid the Republicans open to the charge of seeking by unlawful means to deprive slave-owners of their rights, and it was to the partizan interest of the Democrats to stand by the Court and thus discredit their opponents. This action tended to carry the entire Democratic party to the support of Calhoun's extreme position on the slavery question. Republicans had proclaimed that liberty was national and slavery municipal; that slavery had no warrant for existence except by state enactment; that under the Constitution Congress had no more right to make a slave than it had to make a king; that Congress had no power to establish or permit slavery in the Territories; that it was, on the contrary, the duty of Congress to exclude slavery. On these points the Supreme Court and the Republican party held directly contradictory opinions.

The Democratic platform of 1856 endorsed the

doctrine of popular sovereignty as embodied in the Kansas-Nebraska legislation, which implied that Congress should neither prohibit nor introduce slavery into the Territories, but should leave the inhabitants free to decide that question for themselves, the public domains being open to slave-owners on equal terms with others. But once they had an organized territorial Government and a duly elected territorial Legislature, the residents of a Territory were empowered to choose either slave labor or exclusively free labor. This at least was the view expounded by Stephen A. Douglas, though the theory was apparently rendered untenable by the ruling of the Court which extended protection to slave-owners in all the Territories remaining under the control of the general Government. It followed that if Congress had no power to interfere with that right, much less had a local territorial Government, which is itself a creature of Congress. A state Government alone might control the status of slave property. A Territory when adopting a constitution preparatory to becoming a State would find it then in order to decide whether the proposed State should be free or slave. This was the view held by Jefferson Davis and the extreme pro-slavery leaders. Aided by the authority of the Supreme Court, they were prepared to insist upon a new plank in future Democratic platforms which should guarantee to all slave-owners equal rights in all Territories until they ceased to be Territories. Over this issue the party again divided in 1860.

Republicans naturally imagined that there had been collusion between Democratic politicians and members of the Supreme Court. Mr. Seward made an explicit statement to that effect, and affirmed that President Buchanan was admitted into the secret, alleging as proof a few words in his inaugural address referring to the decision soon to be delivered. Nothing of the sort, however, was ever proven. The historian Von Holst presents the view that there had been a most elaborate and comprehensive program on the part of the slavocracy to control the judiciary of the federal Government. The actual facts, however, admit of a simpler and more satisfactory explanation.

Judges are affected by their environment, as are other men. The transition from the view that slavery was an evil to the view that it is right and just did not come in ways open to general observation, and probably few individuals were conscious of having altered their views. Leading churches throughout the South began to preach the doctrine that slavery is a divinely ordained institution, and by the time of the decision in the Dred Scott case a whole generation had grown up under such teaching.

A large proportion of Southern leaders had become thoroughly convinced of the righteousness of their peculiar system. Not otherwise could they have been so successful in persuading others to accept their views. Even before the Dred Scott decision had crystallized opinion, Franklin Pierce, although a New Hampshire Democrat of anti-slavery traditions, came, as a result of his intimate personal and political association with Southern leaders, to accept their guidance and strove to give effect to their policies. President Buchanan was a man of similar antecedents, and, contrary to the expectation of his Northern supporters, did precisely as Pierce had done. It is a matter of record that the arguments of the Chief Justice had captivated his mind before he began to show his changed attitude towards Kansas. In August, 1857, the President wrote that, at the time of the passage of the Kansas-Nebraska Act, slavery already existed and that it still existed in Kansas under the Constitution of the United States. "This point,"

said he, "has at last been settled by the highest
tribunal known in our laws. How it could ever
have been seriously doubted is a mystery."
Granted that slavery is recognized as a permanent
institution in itself — just and of divine ordinance
and especially united to one section of the country
— how could any one question the equal rights of
the people of that section to occupy with their
slaves lands acquired by common sacrifice? Such
was undoubtedly the view of both Pierce and
Buchanan. It seemed to them "wicked" that
Northern abolitionists should seek to infringe this
sacred right.

By a similar process a majority of the Supreme
Court justices had become converts to Calhoun's
newly announced theory of 1847. It undoubtedly
seemed strange to them, as it did later to President
Buchanan, that any one should ever have held a
different view. If the Court with the force of its
prestige should give legal sanction to the new doctrine, it would allay popular agitation, ensure the
preservation of the Union, and secure to each section its legitimate rights. Such apparently was
the expectation of the majority of the Court in
rendering the decision. But the decision was not
unanimous. Each judge presented an individual

opinion. Five supported the Chief Justice on the main points as to the status of the African race and the validity of the Missouri Compromise. Judge Nelson registered a protest against the entrance of the Court into the political arena. Curtis and McLean wrote elaborate dissenting opinions. Not only did the decision have no tendency to allay party debate, but it added greatly to the acrimony of the discussion. Republicans accepted the dissenting opinions of Curtis and McLean as a complete refutation of the arguments of the Chief Justice; and the Court itself, through division among its members, became a partizan institution. The arguments of the justices thus present a complete summary of the views of the pro-slavery and anti-slavery parties, and the opposing opinions stand as permanent evidence of the impossibility of reconciling slavery and freedom in the same government.

It was through the masterful leadership of Stephen A. Douglas that the Lecompton Constitution was defeated. In 1858 an election was to be held in Illinois to determine whether or not Douglas should be reëlected to the United States Senate. The Buchanan Administration was using its utmost influence to insure Douglas's defeat. Many eastern Republicans believed that in this emergency Illinois Republicans should support Douglas, or at least that they should do nothing to diminish his chances for reëlection; but Illinois Republicans decided otherwise and nominated Abraham Lincoln as their candidate for the senatorship. Then followed the memorable Lincoln-Douglas debates.

This is not the place for any extended account of the famous duel between the rival leaders, but a few facts must be stated. Lincoln had slowly come to the perception that a large portion of the people abhorred slavery, and that the weak point in the armor of Douglas was to be found in the fact that he did not recognize this growing moral sense. Douglas had never been a defender of slavery on ethical grounds, nor had he expressed any distinct aversion to the system. In support of his policy of popular sovereignty his favorite dictum had been, "I do not care whether slavery is voted up or voted down."

This apparent moral obtuseness furnished to Lincoln his great opportunity, for his opponent was apparently without a conscience in respect to the great question of the day. Lincoln, on the contrary, had reached the conclusion not only that slavery was wrong, but that the relation between slavery and freedom was such that they could not be harmonized within the same government. In the debates he again put forth his famous utterance, "A house divided against itself cannot stand," with the explanation that in course of time either this country would become all slave territory or slavery would be restricted and placed in a position which would involve its final extinction. In other words, Lincoln's position was similar to that of the conservative abolitionists. As we know, Birney had given expression to a similar conviction of the impossibility of maintaining both liberty and slavery in this country, but Lincoln spoke at a time when the whole country had been aroused upon the great question; when it was still uncertain whether slavery would not be forced upon the people of Kansas; when the highest court in the land had rendered a decision which was apparently intended to legalize slavery in all Territories; and when the alarming question had been raised whether the next step would not be legalization in all the States.

Lincoln was a long-headed politician, as well as a man of sincere moral judgments. He was defining issues for the campaign of 1860 and was putting Douglas on record so that it would be impossible for him, as the candidate of his party, to become President.   Douglas had many an uncomfortable hour as Lincoln exposed his vain efforts to reconcile his popular sovereignty doctrine with the Dred Scott decision.   As Lincoln expected, Douglas won the senatorship, but he lost the greater prize.

The crusade against slavery was nearing its final stage.   Under the leadership of such men as Sumner, Seward, and Lincoln, a political party was being formed whose policies were based upon the assumption that slavery is both a moral and a political evil.   Even at this stage the party had assumed such proportions that it was likely to carry the ensuing presidential election.   Davis and Yancey, the chief defenders of slavery, were at the same time reaching a definite conclusion as to what should follow the election of a Republican President.   And that conclusion involved nothing less than the fate of the Union.

CHAPTER XIV

JOHN BROWN

THE crusade against slavery was based upon the assumption that slavery, like war, is an abnormal state of society. As the tyrant produces the assassin, so on a larger scale slavery calls forth servile insurrection, or, as in the United States, an implacable struggle between free white persons and the defenders of slavery.

The propaganda of Southern and Western abolitionists had as a primary object the prevention of both servile insurrection and civil war. It was as clear to Southern abolitionists in the thirties as it was to Seward and Lincoln in the fifties that, unless the newly aroused slave power should be effectively checked, a terrible civil war would ensue. To forestall this dreaded calamity, they freely devoted their lives and fortunes. Peaceable emancipation by state action, according to the original program, was prevented by the rise of a sectional animosity which beclouded the issue. As the leadership drifted into the hands of extremists, the conservative masses were confused, misled, or deceived. The South undoubtedly became the victim of the erroneous teachings of alarmists who believed that the anti-slavery North intended, by unlawful and unconstitutional federal action, to abolish slavery in all the States; while the North had equally exaggerated notions as to the aggressive intentions of the South.

The opposing forces finally met on the plains of Kansas, and extreme Northern opposition became personified in John Brown of Osawatomie. He was born in Connecticut in May, 1800, of New England ancestry, the sixth generation from the *Mayflower*. A Calvinist, a mystic, a Bible-reading Puritan, he was trained to anti-slavery sentiments in the family of Owen Brown, his father. He passed his early childhood in the Western Reserve of Ohio, and subsequently moved from Ohio to New York, to Pennsylvania, to Ohio again, to Connecticut, to Massachusetts, and finally to New York once more. He was at various times tanner, farmer, sheep-raiser, horse-breeder, wool-merchant. and a follower of other callings as well. From a business standpoint he may be regarded as a failure, for he had been more than once a bankrupt and involved in much litigation. He was twice married and was the father of twenty children, eight of whom died in infancy.

Until the Kansas excitement nothing had occurred in the history of the Brown family to attract public attention. John Brown was not conspicuous in anti-slavery efforts or in any line of public reform. As a mere lad during the War of 1812 he accompanied his father, who was furnishing supplies to the army, and thus he saw much of soldiers and their officers. The result was that he acquired a feeling of disgust for everything military, and he consistently refused to perform the required military drill until he had passed the age for service. Not quite in harmony with these facts is the statement that he was a great admirer of Oliver Cromwell, and Rhodes says of him that he admired Nat Turner, the leader of the servile insurrection in Virginia, as much as he did George Washington. There seems to be no reason to doubt the testimony of the members of his family that John Brown always cherished a lively interest in the African race and a deep sympathy with them. As a youth he had chosen for a companion a slave boy of his own age, to whom he became greatly

attached. This slave, badly clad and poorly fed,
beaten with iron shovel or anything that came first
to hand, young Brown grew to regard as his equal
if not his superior. And it was the contrast between their respective conditions that first led
Brown to "swear eternal war with slavery." In
later years John Brown, Junior, tells us that, on
seeing a negro for the first time, he felt so great a
sympathy for him that he wanted to take the
negro home with him. This sympathy, he assures
us, was a result of his father's teaching. Upon the
testimony of two of John Brown's sons rests the
oft-repeated story that he declared eternal war
against slavery and also induced the members of
his family to unite with him in formal consecration
to his mission. The time given for this incident
is previous to the year 1840; the idea that he was
a divinely chosen agent for the deliverance of the
slaves was of later development.

As early as 1834 Brown had shown some active
interest in the education of negro children, first in
Pennsylvania and later in Ohio. In 1848 the
Brown family became associated with an enterprise
of Gerrit Smith in northern New York, where a hundred thousand acres of land were offered to negro
families for settlement. During the excitement

over the Fugitive Slave Act of 1850 Brown organized among the colored people of Springfield, Massachusetts, "The United States League of Gileadites." As an organization this undertaking proved a failure, but Brown's formal written instructions to the "Gileadites" are interesting on account of their relation to what subsequently happened. In this document, by referring to the multitudes who had suffered in their behalf, he encouraged the negroes to stand for their liberties. He instructed them to be armed and ready to rush to the rescue of any of their number who might be attacked:

Should one of your number be arrested, you must collect together as quickly as possible, so as to outnumber your adversaries who are taking an active part against you. Let no able-bodied man appear on the ground unequipped, or with his weapons exposed to view: let that be understood beforehand. Your plans must be known only to yourself, and with the understanding that all traitors must die, wherever caught and proven to be guilty. "Whosoever is fearful or afraid, let him return and depart early from Mount Gilead" (Judges, vii. 3; Deut. xx. 8). Give all cowards an opportunity to show it on condition of holding their peace. *Do not delay one moment after you are ready: you will lose all your resolution if you do. Let the first blow be the signal for all to engage: and when engaged do not do your work by halves.*

*but make clean work with your enemies, — and be sure you
meddle not with any others.* By going about your business quietly, you will get the job disposed of before the
number that an uproar would bring together can collect;
and you will have the advantage of those who come out
against you, for they will be wholly unprepared with
either equipments or matured plans; all with them will
be confusion and terror. Your enemies will be slow to
attack you after you have done up the work nicely; and
if they should, they will have to encounter your white
friends as well as you; for you may safely calculate on a
division of the whites, and may by that means get to an
honorable parley.

He gives here a distinct suggestion of the plans and
methods which he later developed and extended.

When Kansas was opened for settlement, John
Brown was fifty-four years old. Early in the spring
of 1855, five of his sons took up claims near Osawatomie. They went, as did others, as peaceable
settlers without arms. After the election of March
30, 1855, at which armed Missourians overawed
the Kansas settlers and thus secured a unanimous
pro-slavery Legislature, the free-state men, under
the leadership of Robinson, began to import
Sharp's rifles and other weapons for defense.
Brown's sons thereupon wrote to their father, describing their helpless condition and urging him to
come to their relief. In October, 1855, John Brown

himself arrived with an adequate supply of rifles
and some broadswords and revolvers. The process
of organization and drill thereupon began, and
when the Wakarusa War occurred early in December, 1855, John Brown was on hand with a small
company from Osawatomie to assist in the defense
of Lawrence. The statement that he disapproved
of the agreement with Governor Shannon which
prevented bloodshed is not in accord with a letter
which John Brown wrote to his wife immediately
after the event. The Governor granted practically
all that the free-state men desired and recognized
their train-bands as a part of the police force of the
Territory. Brown by this stipulation became Captain John Brown, commander of a company of the
territorial militia.

Soon after the Battle of Wakarusa, Captain
Brown passed the command of the company of
militia to his son John, while he became the leader
of a small band composed chiefly of members of
his own family. Writing to his wife on April 7,
1856, he said: "We hear that preparations are
making in the United States Court for numerous
arrests of free-state men. For one I have not
desired (all things considered) to have the slave
power cease from its acts of aggression. 'Their

foot shall slide in due time.'" This letter of
Brown's indicates that the writer was pleased at
the prospect of approaching trouble.

When, six weeks later, notice came of the attack
upon Lawrence, John Brown, Junior, went with
the company of Osawatomie Rifles to the relief
of the town, while the elder Brown with a little
company of six moved in the same direction. In a
letter to his wife, dated June 26, 1856, more than a
month after the massacre in Pottawatomie Valley,
Brown said:

On our way to Lawrence we learned that it had been
already destroyed, and we encamped with John's company overnight. . . . On the second day and evening
after we left John's men, we encountered quite a number of pro-slavery men and took quite a number of
prisoners. Our prisoners we let go, but kept some four
or five horses. We were immediately after this accused
of murdering five men at Pottawatomie and great efforts
have been made by the Missourians and their ruffian
allies to capture us. John's company soon afterwards
disbanded, and also the Osawatomie men. Since then,
we have, like David of old, had our dwelling with
the serpents of the rocks and the wild beasts of the
wilderness.

There will probably never be agreement as to
Brown's motives in slaying his five neighbors on
May 24, 1856. Opinions likewise differ as to the

effect which this incident had on the history of
Kansas. Abolitionists of every class had said much
about war and about servile insurrection, but the
conservative people of the West and South had
mentioned the subject only by way of warning and
that they might point out ways of prevention.
Garrison and his followers had used language which
gave rise to the impression that they favored violent revolution and were not averse to fomenting
servile insurrection. They had no faith in the
efforts of Northern emigrants to save Kansas from
the clutches of the slaveholding South, and they
denounced in severe terms the Robinson leadership there, believing it sure to result in failure. To
this class of abolitionists John Brown distinctly
belonged. He believed that so high was the ten-
sion on the slavery question throughout the country that revolution, if inaugurated at any point,
would sweep the land and liberate the slaves.
Brown was also possessed of the belief that he was
himself the divinely chosen agent to let loose the
forces of freedom; and that this was the chief
motive which prompted the deed at Pottawatomie
is as probable as any other.

Viewed in this light, the Pottawatomie massacre was measurably successful. Opposing forces

became more clearly defined and were pitted against each other in hostile array. There were reprisals and counter-reprisals. Kansas was plunged into a state of civil war, but it is quite probable that this condition would have followed the looting of Lawrence even if John Brown had been absent from the Territory.

Coincident with the warfare by organized companies, small irregular bands infested the country. Kansas became a paradise for adventurers, soldiers of fortune, horse thieves, cattle thieves, and marauders of various sorts. Spoiling the enemy in the interest of a righteous cause easily degenerated into common robbery and murder. It was chiefly in this sort of conflict that two hundred persons were slain and that two million dollars' worth of property was destroyed.

During this period of civil war the members of the Brown family were not much in evidence. John Brown, Junior, captain of the Osawatomie Rifles, was a political prisoner at Topeka. Swift destruction of their property was visited upon all those members who were suspected of having a share in the Pottawatomie murders, and their houses were burned and their other property was seized. Warrants were out for the arrest of the elder Brown and his sons. Captain Pate who, in command of a small troop, was in pursuit of Brown and his company, was surprised at Black Jack in the early morning and induced to surrender. Brown thus gained control of a number of horses and other supplies and began to arrange terms for the exchange of his son and Captain Pate as prisoners of war. The negotiations were interrupted, however, by the arrival of Colonel Sumner with United States troops, who restored the horses and other booty and disbanded all the troops. With the Colonel was a deputy marshal with warrants for the arrest of the Browns. When ordered to proceed with his duty, however, the marshal was so overawed that, even though a federal officer was present, he merely remarked, "I do not recognize any one for whom I have warrants."

After the capture of Captain Pate at Black Jack early in June, little is known about Brown and his troops for two months. Apart from an encounter of opposing forces near Osawatomie in which he and his band were engaged, Brown took no share in the open fighting between the organized companies of opposing forces, and his part in the irregular guerrilla warfare of the period is uncertain. Towards the close of the war one of his sons was shot by a preacher who alleged that he had been robbed by the Browns. After peace had been restored to Kansas by the vigorous action of Governor Geary, Brown left the scene and never again took an active part in the local affairs of the Territory.

John Brown's influence upon the course of affairs in Kansas, like William Lloyd Garrison's upon the general anti-slavery movement of the country, has been greatly misunderstood and exaggerated. Brown's object and intention were fundamentally contradictory to those of the free-state settlers. They strove to build a free commonwealth by legal and constitutional methods. He strove to inaugurate a revolution which would extend to all pro-slavery States and result in universal emancipation. John Brown was in Kansas only one year, and he never made himself at one with those who should have been his fellow-workers but went his solitary way. Only in three instances did he pretend to coöperate with the regular free-state forces. He could not work with them because his conception of the means to be adopted to attain the end was different from theirs. Probably before he left the Territory in 1856, he had realized that his work in Kansas was a failure and that the law-and-order forces were too strong for the execution

of his plans. Certain it is that within a few weeks
after his departure he had transferred the field
of his operations to the mountains of Virginia.
Kansas became free through the persistent determination of the rank and file of Northern settlers
under the wise leadership of Governor Robinson.
It is difficult to determine whether the cause of
Kansas was aided or hindered by the advent of
John Brown and the adventurers with whom his
name became associated.

During the fall of 1856 and until the late summer
of 1857 Brown was in the East raising funds for the
redemption of Kansas and for the reimbursement
of those who had incurred or were likely to incur
losses in defense of the cause. For the equipment
of a troop of soldiers under his own command he
formulated plans for raising $30,000 by private
subscription, and in this he was to a considerable
extent successful. It can never be known how
much was given in this way to Brown for the equipment of his army of liberation. It is estimated
that George L. Stearns alone gave in all fully
$10,000. Because Eastern abolitionists had lost
confidence in Robinson's leadership, they lent a
willing ear to the plea that Captain Brown with a
well-equipped and trained company of soldiers was

the last hope for checking the enemy. Not only would Kansas become a slave State without such help, it was said, but the institution of slavery would spread into all the Territories and become invincible.

The money was given to Brown to redeem Kansas, but he had developed an alternative plan. Early in the year 1857, he met in New York Colonel Hugh Forbes, a soldier of fortune who had seen service with Garibaldi in Italy. They discussed general plans for an aggressive attack upon the South for the liberation of the slaves, and with these plans the needs of Kansas had little or no connection. "Kansas was to be a prologue to the real drama," writes his latest biographer; "the properties of the one were to serve in the other." In April six months' salary was advanced out of the Kansas fund to Forbes, who was employed at a hundred dollars a month to aid in the execution of their plans. Another significant expenditure of the Kansas fund was in pursuance of a contract with a Mr. Blair, a Connecticut manufacturer, to furnish at a dollar each one thousand pikes. Though the contract was dated March 30, 1857, it was not completed until the fall of 1859, when the weapons were delivered to Brown in Pennsylvania for use at Harper's Ferry.

Instead of rushing to the relief of Kansas, as contributors had expected, the leader exercised remarkable deliberation. When August arrived, it found him only as far as Tabor, Iowa, where a considerable quantity of arms had been previously assembled. Here he was joined by Colonel Forbes, and together they organized a school of military tactics with Forbes as instructor. But as Forbes could find no one but Brown and his son to drill, he soon returned to the East, still trusted by Brown as a coworker. It would seem that Forbes himself wished to play the chief part in the liberation of America.

While he was at Tabor, Brown was urged by Lane and other former associates of his in Kansas to come to their relief with all his forces. There had, indeed, been a full year of peace since Geary's arrival, but early in October there was to occur the election of a territorial Legislature in which the free-state forces had agreed to participate, and Lane feared an invasion from Missouri. But although the appeal was not effective, the election proved a complete triumph for the North. Late in October, after the signal victory of the law-and-order party at the election, Brown was again urged with even greater insistence to muster all his forces and come to Kansas, and there were hints in Lane's letter that an aggressive campaign was afoot to rid the Territory of the enemy. Instead of going in force, however, Brown stole into the Territory alone. On his arrival, two days after the date set for a decisive council of the revolutionary faction, he did not make himself known to Governor Robinson or to any of his party but persuaded several of his former associates to join his "school" in Iowa. From Tabor he subsequently transferred the school to Springdale, a quiet Quaker community in Cedar County, Iowa, seven miles from any railway station. Here the company went into winter quarters and spent the time in rigid drill in preparation for the campaign of liberation which they expected to undertake the following season.

While he was at Tabor, Brown began to intimate to his Eastern friends that he had other and different plans for the promotion of the general cause. In January, 1858, he went East with the definite intention of obtaining additional support for the greater scheme. On February 22, 1858, at the home of Gerrit Smith in New York, there was held a council at which Brown definitely outlined his purpose to begin operations at some point in the mountains of Virginia. Smith and Sanborn at first

tried to dissuade him, but finally consented to co-
operate. The secret was carefully guarded: some
half-dozen Eastern friends were apprised of it, including Stearns, their most liberal contributor, and
two or three friends at Springdale.

As early as December, 1857, Forbes began to
write mysterious letters to Sanborn, Stearns, and
others of the circle, in which he complained of ill-
usage at the hands of Brown. It appears that
Forbes erroneously assumed that the Boston
friends were aware of Brown's contract with him
and of his plans for the attack upon Virginia; but,
since they were entirely ignorant on both points,
the correspondence was conducted at cross-pur-
poses for several months. Finally, early in May,
1858, it transpired that Forbes had all the time
been fully informed of Brown's intentions to begin
the effort for emancipation in Virginia. Not only
so, but he had given detailed information on the
subject to Senators Sumner, Seward, Hale, Wilson,
and possibly others. Senator Wilson was told that
the arms purchased by the New England Aid Society for use in Kansas were to be used by Brown
for an attack on Virginia. Wilson, in entire ignorance of Brown's plans, demanded that the Aid
Society be effectively protected against any such

charge of betrayal of trust. The officers of the Society were, in fact, aware that the arms which had been purchased with Society funds the year before and shipped to Tabor, Iowa, had been placed in Brown's hands and that, without their consent, those arms had been shipped to Ohio and just at that time were on the point of being transported to Virginia. This knowledge placed the officers of the New England Aid Society in a most awkward position. Stearns, the treasurer, had advanced large sums to meet pressing needs during the starvation times in Kansas in 1857. Now the arms in Brown's possession were, by vote of the officers, given to the treasurer in part payment of the Society's debt, and he of course left them just where they were.[1] On the basis of this arrangement Senator Wilson and the public were assured that none of the property given for the benefit of Kansas had been or would be diverted to other purposes by the Kansas Committee. It was decided, however, that on account of the Forbes revelations the attack upon Harper's Ferry must be delayed for one year and

[1] "When the dénouement finally came, however, the public and press did not take a very favorable view of the transaction; it was too difficult to distinguish between George L. Stearns, the benefactor of the Kansas Committee, and George L. Stearns, the Chairman of that Committee." — Villard, *John Brown*, p. 341.

that Brown must go to Kansas to take part in the pending elections.

Though Brown arrived in Kansas late in June, he took no active part in the pending measures for the final triumph of the free-state cause. It is something of a mystery how he was occupied between the 1st of July and the middle of December. Under the pseudonym of "Shubal Morgan" he was commander of a small band in which were a number of his followers in training for the Eastern mission. The occupation of this band is not matter of history until December 20, 1858, when they made a raid into the State of Missouri, slew one white man, took eleven slaves, a large number of horses, some oxen, wagons, much food, arms, and various other supplies. This action was in direct violation of a solemn agreement between the border settlers of State and Territory. The people in Kansas were in terror lest retaliatory raids should follow, as would undoubtedly have happened had not the people of Missouri taken active measures to prevent such reprisals.

Rewards were offered for Brown's arrest, and free-state residents served notice that he must leave the Territory. In the dead of winter he started North with some slaves and many horses, accompanied by Kagi and Gill, two of his faithful followers. In northern Kansas, where they were delayed by a swollen stream, a band of horsemen appeared to dispute their passage. Brown's party quickly mustered assistance and, giving chase to the enemy, took three prisoners with four horses as spoils of war. In Kansas parlance the affair is called "The Battle of the Spurs." The leaders in the chase were seasoned soldiers on their way to Harper's Ferry with the intention of spending their lives collecting slaves and conducting them to places of safety. For this sort of warfare they were winning their spurs. It was their intention to teach all defenders of slavery to use their utmost endeavor to keep out of their reach. As Brown and his company passed through Tabor, the citizens took occasion at a public meeting to resolve "that we have no sympathy with those who go to slave States to entice away slaves, and take property or life when necessary to attain that end."

A few days later the party was at Grinnell, Iowa. According to the detailed account which J. B. Grinnell gives in his autobiography, Brown appeared on Saturday afternoon, stacked his arms in Grinnell's parlor and disposed of his people and horses partly in Grinnell's house and barn and

partly at the hotel. In the evening Brown and
Kagi addressed a large meeting in a public hall.
Brown gave a lurid account of experiences in Kansas, justified his raid into Missouri by saying the
slaves were to be sold for shipment to the South,
and gave notice that his surplus horses would be
offered for sale on Monday. "What title can you
give?" was the question that came from the audience. "The best — the affidavit that they were
taken by black men from land they had cleared and
tilled; taken in part payment for labor which is
kept back."

Brown again addressed a large meeting on Sunday evening at which each of the three clergymen
present invoked the divine blessing upon Brown
and his labors. The present writer was told by an
eye-witness that one of the ministers prayed for
forgiveness for any wrongful acts which their guest
may have committed. Convinced of the rectitude
of his actions, however, Brown objected and said
that he thanked no one for asking forgiveness for
anything he had done.

Returning from church on Sunday evening,
Grinnell found a message awaiting him from Mr.
Werkman, United States marshal at Iowa City,
who was a friend of Grinnell. The message in part

read: "You can see that it will give your town a
bad name to have a fight there; then all who aid
are liable, and there will be an arrest or blood. Get
the old Devil away to save trouble, for he will be
taken, dead or alive." Grinnell showed the mes·
sage to Brown, who remarked: "Yes, I have
heard of him ever since I came into the State. . . .
Tell him we are ready to be taken, but will wait
one day more for his military squad." True to his
word he waited till the following afternoon and
then moved directly towards Iowa City, the home
of the marshal, passing beyond the city fourteen
miles to his Quaker friends at Springdale. Here he
remained about two weeks until he had completed
arrangements for shipping his fugitives by rail to
Chicago. In the meantime, where was Marshal
Werkman of Iowa City? Was he of the same mind
as the deputy marshal who had accompanied
Colonel Sumner? Two of Brown's men had visited
the city to make arrangements for the shipment.
The situation was obvious enough to those who
would see. The entire incident is an illuminating
commentary on the attitude of both government
and people towards the Fugitive Slave Law. In
March the fugitives were safely landed in Canada
and the rest of the horses were sold in Cleveland,

Ohio. The time was approaching for the move on Virginia.

Brown now expended much time and attention upon a constitution for the provisional government which he was to set up. In January and February, 1858, Brown had labored over this document for several weeks at the home of Frederick Douglass at Rochester, New York. A copy was in evidence at the conference with Sanborn and Gerrit Smith in February, and the document was approved at a conference held in Chatham, Canada, on May 8, 1858, just at the time when Forbes's revelations caused the postponement of the enterprise. It is an elaborate constitution containing forty-eight articles. The preamble indicates the general purport:

Whereas, Slavery throughout its entire existence in the United States is none other than a most barbarous, unprovoked, and unjustifiable war of one portion of its citizens upon another portion the only conditions of which are perpetual imprisonment and hopeless servitude or absolute extermination; in utter disregard and violation of those eternal and self-evident truths set forth in our Declaration of Independence: *Therefore*, we the citizens of the United States, and the Oppressed People, who, by a decision of the Supreme Court are declared to have no rights which the White Man is bound to respect; together with all other people

degraded by the laws thereof, Do, for the time being
ordain and establish for ourselves, the following PRO-
VISIONAL CONSTITUTION AND ORDINANCES, the better to
protect our Persons, Property, Lives and Liberties and
to govern our actions.

Article Forty-six reads:

The foregoing articles shall not be construed so as in
any way to encourage the overthrow of any State
Government or of the general government of the United
States; and look to no dissolution of the Union, but
simply to Amendment and Repeal. And our flag shall
be the same that our Fathers fought under in the
Revolution.

In Article Forty, "profane swearing, filthy conversation, and indecent behavior" are forbidden.
The document indicates an obvious intention to
effect a revolution by a restrained and regulated
use of force.

Mobilization of forces began in June, 1859.
Cook, one of the original party, had spent the
year in the region of Harper's Ferry. In July the
Kennedy farm, five miles from Harper's Ferry,
was leased. The Northern immigrants posed as
farmers, stock-raisers, and dealers in cattle, seeking a milder climate. To assist in the disguise,
Brown's daughter and daughter-in-law, mere girls,
joined the community. Even so it was difficult to

allay troublesome curiosity on the part of neighbors at the gathering of so many men with no apparent occupation. Suspicion might easily have been aroused by the assembling of numerous boxes of arms from the West and the thousand pikes from Connecticut. Late in August, Floyd, Secretary of War, received an anonymous letter emanating from Springdale, Iowa, giving information which, if acted upon, would have led to an investigation and stopped the enterprise.

The 24th of October was the day appointed for taking possession of Harper's Ferry, but fear of exposure led to a change of plan and the move was begun on the 16th of October. Six of the party who would have been present at the later date were absent. The march from Kennedy farm began about eight o'clock Sunday evening. Before midnight the bridges, the town, and the arsenal were in the hands of the invaders without a gun having been fired. Before noon on Monday some forty citizens of the neighborhood had been assembled as prisoners and held, it was explained, as hostages for the safety of members of the party who might be taken. During the early forenoon Kagi strongly urged that they should escape into the mountains; but Brown, who was influenced, as he said, by sympathy for his prisoners and their distressed families, refused to move and at last found himself surrounded by opposing forces. Brown's men, having been assigned to different duties, were separated. Six of them escaped; others were killed or wounded or taken prisoners. Brown himself with six of his men and a few of his prisoners made a final stand in the engine-house. This was early in the afternoon. All avenues of escape were now closed. Brown made two efforts to communicate with his assailants by means of a flag of truce, sending first Thompson, one of his men, with one of his prisoners, and then Stevens and Watson Brown with another of the prisoners. Thompson was received but was held as a prisoner; Stevens and Watson Brown were shot down, the first dangerously wounded and the other mortally wounded. Later in the afternoon Brown received a flag of truce with a demand that he surrender. He stated the conditions under which he would restore the prisoners whom he held, but he refused the unconditional surrender which was demanded.

About midnight Colonel Robert E. Lee arrived from Washington with a company of marines. He took full command, set a guard of his own men around the engine-house and made preparation to effect a forcible entrance at sunrise on Tuesday morning in case a peaceable surrender was refused. Lee first offered to two of the local companies the honor of storming the castle. These, however, declined to undertake the perilous task, and the honor fell to Lieutenant Green of the marines, who thereupon selected two squads of twelve men each to attempt an entrance through the door. To Lee's aide, Lieutenant Stuart, who had known Brown in Kansas, was committed the task of making the formal demand for surrender. Brown and Stuart, who recognized each other instantly upon their meeting at the door, held a long parley, which resulted, as had been expected, in Brown's refusal to yield. Stuart then gave the signal which had been agreed upon to Lieutenant Green, who ordered the first squad to advance. Failing to break down the door with sledge-hammers, they seized a heavy ladder and at the second stroke made an opening near the ground large enough to admit a man. Green instantly entered, rushed to the back part of the room, and climbed upon an engine to command a better view. Colonel Lewis Washington, the most distinguished of the prisoners, pointed to Brown, saying, "This is Osawatomie." Green leaped forward and by thrust or stroke bent

his light sword double against Brown's body.
Other blows were administered and his victim fell
senseless, and it was believed that the leader had
been slain in action according to his wish.

The first of the twelve men to attempt to follow
their leader was instantly killed by gunshot.
Others rushed in and slew two of Brown's men by
the use of the bayonet. To save the prisoners from
harm, Lee had given careful instruction to fire no
shot, to use only bayonets. The other insurgents
were made prisoners. "The whole fight," Green
reported, "had not lasted over three minutes."

Of all the prisoners taken and held as hostages,
not one was killed or wounded. They were made
as safe as the conditions permitted. The eleven
prisoners who were with Brown in the engine-
house were profoundly impressed with the courage,
the bearing, and the self-restraint of the leader and
his men. Colonel Washington describes Brown as
holding a carbine in one hand, with one dead son
by his side, while feeling the pulse of another son,
who had received a mortal wound, all the time
watching every movement for the defense and
forbidding his men to fire upon any one who was
unarmed. The testimony is uniform that Brown
exercised special care to prevent his men from

shooting unarmed citizens, and this conduct was undoubtedly influential in securing generous treatment for him and his men after the surrender.

For six weeks afterwards, until his execution on the 2d of December, John Brown remained a conspicuous figure. He won universal admiration for courage, coolness, and deliberation, and for his skill in parrying all attempts to incriminate others. Probably less than a hundred people knew beforehand anything about the enterprise, and less than a dozen of these rendered aid and encouragement. It was emphatically a personal exploit. On the part of both leader and followers, no occasion was omitted to drive home the lesson that men were willing to imperil their lives for the oppressed with no hope or desire for personal gain. Brown especially served notice upon the South that the day of final reckoning was at hand.

It is natural that the consequences of an event so spectacular as the capture of Harper's Ferry should be greatly exaggerated. Brown's contribution to Kansas history has been distorted beyond all recognition. The Harper's Ferry affair, however, because it came on the eve of the final election before the war, undoubtedly had considerable influence. It sharpened the issue. It played into the hands of extremists in both sections. On one side, Brown was at once made a martyr and a hero; on the other, his acts were accepted as a demonstration of Northern malignity and hatred, whose fitting expression was seen in the incitement of slaves to massacre their masters.

The distinctive contribution of John Brown to American history does not consist in the things which he did but rather in that which he has been made to represent. He has been accepted as the personification of the irrepressible conflict.

Of all the men of his generation John Brown is best fitted to exemplify the most difficult lesson which history teaches: that slavery and despotism are themselves forms of war, that the shedding of blood is likely to continue so long as the rich, the strong, the educated, or the efficient, strive to force their will upon the poor, the weak, and the ignorant. Lincoln uttered a final word on the subject when he said that no man is good enough to rule over another man; if he were good enough he would not be willing to do it.

BIBLIOGRAPHICAL NOTE

AMONG the many political histories which furnish a background for the study of the anti-slavery crusade, the following have special value:

J. F. Rhodes, *History of the United States from the Compromise of 1850*, 7 vols. (1893–1906). The first two volumes cover the decade to 1860. This is the best-balanced account of the period, written in an admirable judicial temper. H. E. von Holst, *Constitutional and Political History of the United States*, 8 vols. (1877–1892). A vast mine of information on the slavery controversy. The work is vitiated by an almost virulent antipathy toward the South. James Schouler, *History of the United States*, 7 vols. (1895–1901). A sober, reliable narrative of events. Henry Wilson, *History of the Rise and Fall of the Slave Power in America*, 3 vols. (1872–1877). The fullest account of the subject, written by a contemporary. The material was thrown together by an overworked statesman and lacks proportion.

Three volumes in the *American Nation Series* aim to combine the treatment of special topics of commanding interest with general political history. A. B. Hart's *Slavery and Abolition* (1906) gives an account of the origin of the controversy and carries the history down to 1841. G. P. Garrison's *Westward Extension* (1906)

deals especially with the Mexican War and its results.
T. C. Smith's *Parties and Slavery* (1906) follows the
gradual disruption of parties under the pressure of the
slavery controversy.

From the mass of contemporary controversial literature a few titles of more permanent interest may be
selected. William Goodell's *Slavery and Anti-Slavery*
(1852) presents the anti-slavery arguments. A. T.
Bledsoe's *An Essay on Liberty and Slavery* (1856) and
The Pro-Slavery Argument (1852), a series of essays by
various writers, undertake the defense of slavery.

Only a few of the biographies which throw light on the
crusade can be mentioned. *William Lloyd Garrison*, 4
vols. (1885–1889) is the story of the editor of the *Libera-
tor* told exhaustively by his children. Less voluminous
but equally important are the following: W. Birney,
James G. Birney and His Times (1890); G. W. Julian,
Joshua R. Giddings (1892); Catherine H. Birney, *Sarah
and Angelina Grimké* (1885); John T. Morse, *John
Quincy Adams.* Those who have not patience to read
E. L. Pierce's ponderous *Memoir and Letters of Charles
Sumner*, 4 vols. (1877–1893), would do well to read G. H.
Haynes's *Charles Sumner* (1909).

The history of the conflict in Kansas is closely associated with the lives of two rival candidates for the
honor of leadership in the cause of freedom. James Red-
path in his *Public Life of Captain John Brown* (1860),
Frank B. Sanborn in his *Life and Letters of John Brown*
(1885), and numerous other writers give to Brown the
credit of leadership. The opposition view is held by
F. W. Blackmar in his *Life of Charles Robinson* (1902),
and by Robinson himself in his *Kansas Conflict* (2d ed.,
1898). The best non-partizan biography of Brown is

O. G. Villard's *John Brown, A Biography Fifty Years After* (1910).

The Underground Railroad has been adequately treated in W. H. Siebert's *The Underground Railroad from Slavery to Freedom* (1898), but Levi Coffin's *Reminiscences* (1876) gives an earlier autobiographical account of the origin and management of an important line, while Mrs. Stowe's *Uncle Tom's Cabin* throws the glamour of romance over the system.

For additional bibliographical information the reader is referred to the articles on *Slavery, Fugitive Slave Laws, Kansas, William Lloyd Garrison, John Brown, James Gillespie Birney,* and *Frederick Douglass* in *The Encyclopædia Britannica* (11th Edition).

INDEX

Abolition party, 96

Abolitionists, in theory and practice, 9; state policy, 10; societies established, 11; character of societies, 12–13; of middle section, 18–20; against war, 52; division among New England, 57; extreme attitude, 60; of South, 68; legislation against, 71–72, 83; hearing in Massachusetts, 72–74; Methodist Church opposes (1836), 74; mail controversy, 75–78; right of petition, 78–82; mob violence against, 83; cause furthered by opposition, 85; propaganda suppressed in South, 86; theory as to rights of Congress, 101; connection with Underground Railroad, 114; stigmatized as lawbreakers, 130; aim, prevention of civil war, 203; *see also* Anti-slavery societies, Emancipation

Adams, J. Q., on right of petition, 78–82; warns South, 85–86; against extension of slavery, 86–87; successors, 99–100, 165

Alabama admitted as State (1819), 15; forbids importation of slaves, 35; Birney as educational leader in, 35; Williams indicted in, 70

American and Foreign Anti-Slavery Society, 57

American Anti-Slavery Society,

Birney's connection with, 36–37; in Philadelphia, 45–46; women and, 45–46, 49, 57; recognizes division of state and federal powers, 56

American Colonization Society, Birney contributes to, 34–35

Anthony, Susan B., 51–52

"Anti-Nebraska men," 149–50

Anti-Slavery Friends Society, 121–22

Anti-slavery societies, 94; *see also* Abolitionists, American and Foreign Anti-Slavery Society, American Anti-Slavery Society, Anti-Slavery Friends Society, Colonization, New England Anti-Slavery Society, New York Anti-Slavery Society, Pennsylvania Abolition Society

Arkansas becomes slave State (1836), 17

Atchison, D. R., 146, 147, 148

Baptist Church, division in, 84

"Barnburners," 92

Barnes, Jack, slave case, 115–16

Beecher, H. W., 157–58

"Beecher's Bibles," 158

Benton, T. H., 145, 146, 147

Birney, J. G., born (1792), 33; early life, 33–34; favors gradual emancipation, 34–35; removes to Alabama, 34; educational leader, 35; interviews Clay, 35, 90; agent of colonization society, 36; returns to

237